The Media on *This is True* . . . .

"How did he get so popular so fast? Well, for one thing, he writes funny stuff."

New York Times

"One of our favorite [online features]. If you like what you read, buy the book."

Internet World

"'This is True' [is] filled with interesting off-beat news stories culled from newspapers and wire services."

United Press International

Randy Cassingham is "A humorist for the Information Age, an Internet-savvy satirist and social commentator. The Jay Leno of Cyberspace."

Los Angeles Times

"And now for something completely different."

CNN Morning News

"One of the most popular Internet sites in the World."

KEX-AM (Portland, OR)

"If you can't make it home to watch the weird perversions of society on the Sally Jesse Oprah Geraldo Povich show, try **This is True**."

The Whole Internet Calendar

Randy Cassingham is "The [David] Letterman of the Net."

MediaTelevision (CityTV, Toronto)

"Written with dry humor."

Nihon Keizai Shimbun (the "*Nikkei*")

What *True*'s Readers Say . . . .

"One of the most consistently intelligent and humorous collections of writing I've ever seen!"

Vince, Washington DC

"I loved your first book! Then a 'friend' of mine stole it. I just had to buy two more copies to make sure I would always have one."

Marco, Italy

"I am only 13 years old, but I just can't get enough of these weird, funny, and true news articles."

Edward, California

"It brightens up my day every time I read about someone else in the world who does 'dumb' things. You sure come up with them!"

Nancy, Michigan

"[You] are providing weekly yuks to the overworked staff of the U.S. Embassy in New Delhi. Thanks."

Steve, India

"The articles you report are great, but it's your comments after each that really make the difference."

Mike, Virginia

"There is no better morning than my 'This is True' morning."

Hans, Belgium

"As someone who worked on a newspaper copy desk and wrote more than my share of headlines under deadline, I have to tell you that your headlines are *great*. I'm impressed, amused, and inspired."

Ellie, California

This is True:
Glow-in-Dark Plants Could Help Farmers
And 500 Other Bizarre-but-True Stories
and Headlines From the World's Press

The *This is True* Collection, Volume Two

This is True:
Glow-in-Dark Plants Could Help Farmers
And 500 Other Bizarre-but-True Stories
and Headlines From the World's Press

The *This is True* Collection, Volume Two

---

by

Randy Cassingham

Freelance Communications
Boulder, Colorado

"This is True" is a trademark of Freelance Communications

Published by Freelance Communications
  Post Office Box 17326
  Boulder, Colorado, 80308 USA
  (500) 448-TRUE (448-8783) • Fax (500) 442-TRUE (442-8783)

9 8 7 6 5 4 3 2 1

Printed and bound in the United States of America using non-petroleum ink on acid-free paper.

International Standard Book Number: 0-935309-22-5

Preface . . . .

Welcome to the the second *This is True* collection. *True* is a weekly
collection of bizarre-but-true news stories with running commen-
tary, plus an actual "headline of the week", that is sold to newspapers and magazines as a feature column. (The first collection,
This is True: Deputy Kills Man With Hammer, is still available
— see your bookseller, or the last page of this book, to get a copy.

I like to make it clear what is it I mean by "true". *True*'s stories
don't come from the tabloids or underground newspapers, but
rather from the legitimate/mainstream print media, such as national and international news wires, city newspapers, and major
newsweeklies like *Newsweek.* But let me caution you: take everything you read in newspapers — and even in *This is True* — with
at least a small grain of salt. In addition to my job as a writer, I've
worked a few other careers, including a brief stint as a sheriff
deputy, several years as a paramedic, and nearly ten years at a
NASA field center. One thing in common in all of these jobs is
that I have often been a participant in, or direct observer of, events
that tend to end up on the news or in the paper. And not once,
when I knew the entire story, did any news report on the event
come without at least some small error in the "facts".

So I watch carefully for corrections. Whenever I've discovered that
an item in *This is True* was based on a "fact" taken in error, or
indeed if I've made an error myself, the item has been corrected.
But I have resisted the temptation to improve (beyond grammar
or typos) my comments — they are as they were written under
deadline pressure.

In addition to the print outlets that carry *This is True,* readers can
subscribe and get it on the Internet. For details on that, please see
<http://www.thisistrue.com>. You'll be happy to note that even
if you've read True every week online — or in print — you still
have not read every story in this book. I very often have leftover
stories which don't fit in the weekly column (it does have a word

limit). Some weeks have them, some don't, but there are quite a few stories mixed in throughout, plus a section of leftover head-lines at the end. Fortunately for me, there is never a shortage of material about the weird things we humans do.

The stories for *This is True* come from "legitimate" printed news media, both American and international. I try as much as possible to credit the original source. For example, if a story is taken from a newspaper, but the newspaper credits a wire service as the source, I do too — I don't necessarily credit the paper I found the story in. Thus the most-cited sources in this book are the major news wires:

- AP (Associated Press)
- Reuter (Reuters Ltd.)
- UPI (United Press International)

This volume compiles columns released to syndication from June, 1995 through the end of July, 1996.

Last: my friends sometimes express worry about me. They think that writing stories like these week after week might mean I'm a cynic. I state for the record that I am not a cynic; I am a frustrated idealist.

Randy Cassingham
Boulder, Colorado

Edited by Robert Nelson
Book and Cover Design by Freelance Communications

For my brother Curt,
who "gets it".

"There is nothing so powerful as the truth, and nothing so strange."
Daniel Webster (1782–1852)

A Day at the Office: Apparently there's not enough to do on the Shanghai Stock Exchange's trading floor. In addition to banning alcoholic beverages, recent rules have been issued to keep traders from smoking, gambling, eating, playing cards, sleeping and "joking around". And playing chess. And knitting sweaters. (Reuter) ...*A formal reprimand? But this is cross stitch!*

Reduce, Reuse, Recycle: The California State Cemetery Board is investigating a cemetery in Santa Fe Springs, near downtown Los Angeles. About 200 grave markers, as well as numerous bones and pieces of old coffins, have been found in a dirt pile there, suggesting that graves have been dug up to be resold to new occupants — perhaps as many as eight times. Raymond Giunta, the Board's executive officer, said it would be impossible to identify individual remains so they could be reburied, so all of the bones will be put into a mass grave. (AP) ...*That's the kind of problem that could come back to haunt you.*

Just Do It Until You Need Glasses: The University of Pittsburgh's Eye and Ear Institute has lent scientific validity to the concept that intense sexual activity can cause blindness — at least temporarily. Dr. Thomas Friberg reports that intense sex can lead to a "spike" in blood pressure, which can cause a hemorrhage in the eye. "This is really rare, considering the amount of sexual activity that goes on, but I would assume there are other patients out there who just don't report it," he said. (AP) ...*Of course not — it would be tantamount to conceding that the nuns at their elementary school were right.*

It's Not Just Science, It's the Law: One of the oldest corollaries of Murphy's Law has been proven by physicist Robert Matthews of Aston University in Birmingham, England: he indeed found that "toast falling off the breakfast table lands butter side down because the universe is made that way," he said after practical tests backed up by mathematical modeling. Actually, it's the top side that ends up face down, whether it's buttered or not, but most people do butter the top side. (Reuter) ...*But of course, if you strap buttered toast to the back of a cat and then drop it, it will float* *indefinitely.*

Jingle Bells: The Santa Claus House, a year-round Christmas shop in the town of North Pole, Alaska, is in need of a few good men. Especially fat, jolly men. But no one wants the full time job of playing Santa Claus for tourists, so currently a mannequin is sitting in Santa's big chair. "We just detour them to the reindeer" if a tourist comes in looking for Saint Nick, says store clerk Angela Rickels. The job pays $7.50 an hour, and the applicant must be willing to greet tour busses, shout "ho ho ho", and listen to children's gift requirements through the summer season. (AP) *...Children are forgiving. Just tell them he's at the Betty Ford Clinic, getting in touch with his inner self. They'll understand.*

Jingle Bells II: Meanwhile, a man in New Zealand has been convicted in Wellington for punching out a security window at a service station. In December, Michael Lindsay had played Santa at a party and stopped for some ice cream on the way home. Still wearing his suit, he became enraged when the clerk wouldn't give him the ice cream for free and smashed his fist through the window. He's been sentenced to six months of "periodic detention" and fined NZ$134. (Reuter) *...Ah, good: out just in time for Christmas!*

Honesty in Government: It has long been a tradition to make available to the public American flags that "have flown" over the U.S. Capitol. But they have become so popular that there are now three full-time Capitol employees running 500 flags up the pole per day to satisfy demand. To make sure the employees actually run the flags up the pole, and not just open the boxes and show them to the sky, that Architect of the Capitol George White has installed a security camera so that the employees know they are being watched. (Reuter) *...As long as Big Brother only watches himself, we may not have a problem.*

Corporate Merger: Three churches in Pewaukee, Wis. — one each Catholic, Episcopalian and Lutheran — are considering joining together into one church. "We can't share Communion, but practically everything else we can do together," noted the Rev. Richard Dick of the Lutheran church. "I think of it as a cinema triplex, with common areas and chapels of your choosing," said the Rev. Brian Beno of the Catholic church. "This (sounds) like a real opportunity." (AP) *...Naw, I don't want to see that sermon. Let's go see "Sodom and Gomorrah" again.*

Hold Still So I Can Pollinate You: Mychal Limric, a television news reporter from station KVEW, was attempting to report a story on beekeeping in Kennewick, Wash., when the bees started to attack his head. Neither the beekeeper nor Limric's cameraman, Dao Vu, were attacked. The difference? To look good on camera, Limric's hair was kept neat with hair gel. (AP) *...Either that, or they recognized him.*

What Would You Expect?
Kevorkian's Clinic Short-Lived
AP headline

Refused Booze: Systembolaget, the state alcoholic beverage distributor in Sweden, has refused to distribute "TNT Liquid Dynamite" cider. The drink is packaged in orange tubes decorated with fuses so that the containers look like sticks of dynamite. "This is a bit too much for the Swedish market," a Systembolaget spokesman said. "You are led to believe that it is something you drink to get absolutely smashed, that is has a dynamite effect." (Reuter) *...Which is false advertising, since we drank several without getting bombed.*

Give Them an Inch, and They'll Confiscate It: Alabama prison commissioner Ron Jones has ordered that vegetable gardens and potted plants being grown by prisoners be destroyed. "We have never allowed inmates in our prisons to have potted plants," Jones said. "Today it's tomatoes and tomorrow it's marijuana and God knows what else." (AP) *...Liar. He just didn't want them to have any food with flavor.*

Prison Food II: Two prisoners in Rubtsovsk, Russia, allegedly said they wanted "to add some spice to their life," so they strangled their cellmate, cooked some of his body parts over a fire made by burning a blanket, and ate him. "Medical experts" have judged the two sane, so they have been charged with murder. (Reuter) ...*If only they had been allowed to grow a few vegetables, they would be productive citizens today.*

There They Go Again: By the end of June, 141 potential candidates had registered with the U.S. Federal Election Commission for the 1996 presidential election — nowhere near the record of 273 registrants in 1992, "but it's early yet," Reuter notes. Not all of the presidential hopefuls are people you may have heard of. For instance, immediately next to Bill Clinton on the Commission's alphabetical list is Billy Joe "Won't Pull Your Leg" Clegg, supported by his Biloxi, Miss., "Just Kaus" presidential campaign committee. (Reuter) ...*On the other hand, most of us have never heard of some of the mainstream party candidates either.*

Thank You, Please Come Again: Amir Brikho, 38, needed some cash. So he stopped at Valle de Oro Bank in La Mesa, Calif., and made a large withdrawal. The teller gave Brikho the cash, but as he left the bank he heard a loud bang — the teller had accidentally given him a special packet of bills loaded with dye and tear gas that's supposed to be given to robbers. "I thought somebody shot me," Brikho said. Then he noticed "smoke was coming from my shorts." After being treated for burns at a local hospital, Brikho notes "now it is funny, but at the time it was serious." (AP) ...*When he sees the bank's fee for the packet he used, it'll be serious again.*

Carried Away: Two centuries ago, Ronkainen the Robber tested new gang recruits by making them carry a woman over an obstacle course to show that they could carry handle their loot — they often stole wives from other tribes. But in modern Sonkajarvi, Finland, it's known as the Finnish National Wife-Carrying Championships. The goal: carry a woman, preferably someone else's wife (and she must be older than 17) over a 780-foot course through water, sand, grass and asphalt, and over two fences. Dropping the wife results in a 15-second penalty. The fastest man earns the big prize: the woman's weight in lemonade. "We Finns can be mad without alcohol, too, you know," said one local, attempting to explain the prize — beer was ruled illegal. "This is very, very Finnish," agreed a Swedish woman who was carried in the race. "They wouldn't do this in Sweden." (Reuter) ... *What, the race, or the prize?*

Finn Contest II: Meanwhile, in Pelkosenniemi, Finland, the third World Championship of Mosquito Killing has begun. Contestants have five minutes to kill as many of the buzzy pests as possible, but only using their bare hands. This year, the warm, moist summer season will probably mean last year's record — seven — will be beaten. "I know it's surprisingly few, but the problem is that the mosquitoes are drawn [away] by the warmth of the crowd watching the competition," noted Kai Kullervo Salmijarvi, who organized this year's event. While insecticides are banned, "we don't have dope tests," he added, "so anyone can tank up as they see fit." (AP) ...*Let's see: no beer for prizes, but they can go hunting while on dope. Got it.*

Honor Among Thieves: Michael Smith, 30, was in the process of robbing a betting shop in London when his partner, who has not been named, suddenly decided that the robbery wasn't a good idea. The co-conspirator arrested Smith, who had just relieved the shop of 760 pounds, and held him in a headlock until police arrived. Smith has been sentenced to 2.5 years in prison. The accomplice was not charged with any crimes for "obvious reasons," the judge said. (Reuter) ...*Good thing Smith was convicted, or his friend would probably have been charged with false arrest.*

Type Oh: Moon God Drinking Products Co., a skin care products company in China, has offered a bounty of 1,000 yuan (US$120) for every typographical or literary error found in a day's editions of four Chinese publications in an attempt to embarrass journalists into better writing. Hao Mingjian, who came up with the idea for the bounty, said that "China's press has lost its polish in the past decade or two," which "reflects a chaotic cultural environment and shows people lack a sense of responsibility." (Reuter) ...*Nice try, but journalists can't be embarrassed.*

Bummer
Chinese Woman Told
She's Actually a Man
Reuter headline

Down Boy! The U.S. Food and Drug Administration has approved a new drug to treat impotence. The drug is injected into the base of the penis and usually results in an erection within 5–20 minutes. One side effect: sometimes the erection doesn't go away. Men are warned not to use the drug more than once a day nor more than three times per week. "Caverject" should be available in September, said the company that markets it: Upjohn. (AP) *...Somehow it figures that it has to be injected, rather than rubbed vigorously into the skin.*

Rescue Dog: While Hannah Wilson was at work, her terrier puppy, Jemima, found the telephone. The Leytonstone, England, dog pulled the phone onto the floor and started pawing the buttons. It managed to dial 999, the emergency number. Apparently hearing nothing but panting on the other end of the call, dispatchers sent police to investigate. Since there was no answer at the door, police broke through the sturdy door with sledgehammers, fearing the caller had collapsed into unconsciousness. "I've forgiven Jemima. It was just a freak accident," Wilson said. She's asking police to help pay for the broken door. (Reuter) *...It's her own fault if she didn't train the dog to answer the door after he's invited someone over.*

Stop That: An administrative law judge has issued an order to Harold Weingold of West Orange, N.J., to stop promising that a $15 "cosmic protector" that he's advertising will bring buyers good luck and protect them from bad people. The judge noted the protector "is actually a solar-powered calculator." Cosmic powers? No, it "has no inherent power to do anything but assist the user in performing mathematical calculations," she ruled. (AP) *...Seems to me that if people buy one, it has already not worked.*

Legal Hearing: Dutch police have gone back to basics. While some investigators are making strides with DNA typing, police in the Netherlands have expanded basic fingerprinting technology — to ear prints. Apparently, some burglars listen at doors and windows before breaking in, leaving behind a clear impression of their ears. Several convictions have been made on the basis of the ear evidence. (Reuter) ...*Next: nose printing in cocaine cases.*

This Arrest Brought to You By: The city council in Oxnard, Calif., has approved a plan to allow advertising space to be sold on city police cars. "We think the public safety vehicle could attract a lot of attention for businesses," the police chief said. Fees for ad space would help pay for the cars. A local newspaper made fun of the plan by suggesting the cars could display the slogan for Taco Bell: "Make a run for the border." (AP) ...*Surely, then, WonderBra could sponsor some of the smaller busts.*

Who Goes There? An Egyptian policeman was standing guard at a checkpoint in Malawi, which is under a strict curfew. When a private car driven by a police captain in civilian clothes drove through the checkpoint without stopping, the policeman opened fire. For strictly adhering to his orders and shooting his captain, the policeman has been rewarded with the equivalent of US$29. The captain was seriously wounded. (Reuter) ...*Makes you wonder: did he shoot because he didn't know who the driver was, or because he did?*

Home Business: Piet van Schijndel, who operates a draw bridge in the Netherlands, loves his job of 20 years. The bridge he tends is being replaced, so he bought it and is having it installed in his Heeswijk back yard. "I just think it's a beautiful bridge," he said. "I have room at home." After the rebuilding job is complete, he'll add a pond to the yard. "A bridge has to have water under it," he explained. (AP) ...*And his wife thought a bridge tender never brought his work home with him.*

Stoned: Lawrence Shields of Alexandria, Va., was on vacation with his parents in Franklin, N.C., when they stopped at a gemstone mine. As a gimmick, tourists can buy a bucket of dirt from the mine, paw through it, and keep anything they find. The

10-year-old found a 1,061-carat blue sapphire in his bucket, one of the largest ever found in the state. When bystanders got excited and took pictures, the boy's mother "thought it was because he was a little kid," she said. "We thought, 'These people in the mountains are really nice'." The $35,000 rock might help to pay for Lawrence's education, his father said. But "I've decided to buy a fishing boat," Lawrence retorted. (AP) ...*Now there's a kid who has his priorities straight!*

Whenever You're Ready: An Indian citizen put in a visa application at the U.S. Embassy in New Delhi so he could travel to the U.S. to attend former President Ronald Reagan's funeral. When told that Reagan is still alive, he replied "I am aware of that. [But] I would rather wait there than here." It is unclear whether the man received his visa. (Reuter) ...*Somehow, I think he deserves one.*

What Did You Learn at School Today?

Noisy Kids Drive Teacher to Wrist-Slashing

Reuter headline

Go Down in History: The 1000th known suicide off San Francisco's Golden Gate Bridge was recorded this month. The California Highway Patrol, which tallies the statistics, had tried to keep a low profile on the upcoming milestone after their experience with a previous milestone. As number 500 approached in 1973, authorities were able to stop 14 jumpers in a row, including one man wearing a t-shirt reading "500". But this year, area media would not cooperate with the low key approach: the count was widely known, and one local radio station offered prizes to the 1000th jumper. (AP) ...*Which will be awarded just as soon as number 1000 comes in to claim them.*

If It Tastes Good, It Must be Bad for You: Philippine Catholic Bishop Jesus Varela is leading a protest against a local sales of "diabolical" strawberry-flavored condoms. "This will encourage oral sex," he said. "Condoms don't belong to the taste buds." DKT International said its flavored condoms are just another way to help prevent AIDS. What other ways are there? "We're looking at mint, which seems to be a popular flavor in Asia. We're looking at chocolate mocha. You can have any flavor you like," a DKT spokesman said. (Reuter) *...Then how about "Neapolitan"?*

Wrong Turn: Three teens heading to the beach in St. Lucie, Fla., took a shortcut through the grounds of the local power plant. But their four-wheel-drive vehicle slid down an embankment, ended up in the nuke plant's water discharge canal, and was swept away in the water. "It was real warm, like, you know, a hot tub," Tim Svane, 17, said later. The vehicle ended up plugging a pipe a quarter-mile away, but all three were able to swim to safety. "I took a swimming class last semester in high school, and I was saying, 'Thank you, thank you, thank you' to my swimming coach all the way to the edge," Svane said. (AP) *...See? We told you that your high school lessons can be applied to real life situations.*

Odd Couple: "I feel pretty stupid," said Bruce Jensen, 39, of Bountiful, Utah. His wife was arrested on fraud charges, and police had to break it to him that his wife of 3-1/2 years was a man, Felix Urioste. The two were married after Urioste told Jensen "she" was pregnant with twins by Jensen — she later told him the twins were stillborn. The bishop of Jensen's Mormon church confirms that Jensen is "just a little country bumpkin from Wyoming." Jensen has filed for an annulment of the marriage based on irreconcilable differences and has left Bountiful, but he told a newspaper that when the case is over, he plans to return to Wyoming, "crawl in a hole for a few years and not let anyone within rifle range." (AP) *...Life Lesson number 2: never marry anyone without seeing them naked first.*

The Musical Fruit: Peas and Beans Ltd, a British research firm, cannot get grants to study their founder's field of expertise: flatulence. To get something going, P&B has teamed up with M-scan, a company that makes "highly efficient chemical sniffing equipment," says P&B's Dr. Colin Leakey. Dr. Leakey thus used a "flatometer" to discover that "there is about a 10:1 difference in the flatus gas of acetone and 2-propanol." His research helped him develop a new variety of bean that appears "to have higher digestibility and lower flatulence." (Reuter) ...*Maybe we can adapt the flatometer to help size up politicians.*

The Musical Animal: The British Ecological Society, studying the apparent upswing in songbirds being unable to sing on key, has decided that loud noises from auto traffic is to blame. The Society says that many wrens, tits, woodcock and pheasant are now unable to use their calls to scare away intruders or attract mates, and says that the many roads of the British countryside are the culprit. "This is proof of what we have long suspected, that roads and birds do not mix," Said a British Trust for Ornithology spokesman. (Reuter) ...*Then why are they always aiming for my car?*

Home Run: In 1956, Nick George Montos became the first man ever to be on the FBI's "Ten Most Wanted" list twice, and has been running from the law for nine years. But the fugitive met his match: Sonia Paine, the 73-year-old owner of an antique shop he tried to rob. Montos, 78, had tied Paine up and was ripping the store off when she was able to break free, trip an alarm, and hit Montos over the head with a baseball bat. "I don't take any crap from anybody," Paine said. "I beat the hell out of him." It wasn't an easy struggle: she hit him three times, but he was able to get the bat and hit her, and he sprayed her with tear gas before she was able to get the upper hand. Paine, who is from Poland, likes the U.S. "What a beautiful country, but filled with a lot of awful people, honey." (AP) ...*Not all of us, sweetheart. Not all of us.*

Finally Figured it Out

Waist Measurement Holds Key to Obesity —UK Doctors

Reuter headline

Foul Ball: The state of Maine's Supreme Judicial Court has upheld a $40,000 award to a golfer who was hit by her own ball. Jeannine Pelletier's drive bounced off nearby railroad tracks — which are visible from the tee — and hit her in the face. The court ruled that despite the fact the Fort Kent Golf Club did not own the tracks, "the club's duty extends to land which it has invited golfers to use." (AP) ...*These lawsuits are getting out of hand. Someone should sue to stop them.*

Another Blooming Idea: British gardeners take their sport seriously. With grass in town browned by a severe heat wave, officials in Stroud, England, knew they'd have trouble winning the "Britain in Bloom" competition. So, with just hours to spare before judges were due to arrive, they sprayed the parched grass with green dye. "I was gobsmacked when I saw what they were doing," one local said. "I think it's bloody ridiculous." But one of the organizers noted "the Britain in Bloom competition has rules against artificial flowers, but I don't think it says anything about dyed grass." (Reuter) ...*I'm sure all of us are gobsmacked by this turn of events.*

We're Number One! Edmund Donoghue, the medical examiner in Cook County, Ill., is under fire for classifying too many deaths as "heat-related" in a nationwide wave of hot weather. Because of their liberal labeling of deaths as heat-related, the number of Chicago-area victims has been put well into the hundreds — at least half of the national toll. "There's no uniform federal definition for heat-related deaths," confirmed a spokeswoman for the federal Centers for Disease Control and Prevention — it's up to the medical examiners to choose how to classify deaths. "We're confident that we're going to be upheld on this," Donoghue said in a recent press conference. (AP) ...*What: the Bulls don't win for once, so someone else has to replace the glory?*

Signs of a Problem: "Raymond Ward Tells Lies" read one sign put up by Alan Kingston in his Kempston, England, neighborhood. "Ward the Fraud" said another. Kingston's car bore a sign that noted "We have no connection with the liar, con man, bankrupt who lives at 57." Ray Ward, who has lived in the same house for 28 years, wasn't sure what else to do about Kingston, his next door neighbor for just four years, so he sued him. On Wednesday, Kingston was ordered to pay Ward 1000 pounds in libel damages — plus about 20,000 pounds for Ward's legal costs. Kingston says he may have to sell his house to pay the award. (AP) ...*Well, then, the problem looks well solved.*

Marked for Life: Four adults in Nebraska have been released from charges of felony child abuse for allowing their daughters to get tattoos. Prosecutors failed to show that any harm had come to the girls, who are aged 11 to 13. All had consented to the procedures. (AP) ...*Not so fast: we just noticed they have pierced ears, too!*

Optional Security Feature: When Carl Reese carjacked a Lexus in Coral Springs, Fla., he stuffed the car's owner, Paul Brite, in the trunk at gunpoint and drove off. Then, he thought, what if there was a portable phone in that trunk that the victim could use to call for help? Reese pulled over and opened the trunk to check. Brite didn't have a phone stored in the trunk, but he did have two guns there. "He ordered the suspect several times to lie on the ground, firing two warning shots," a police spokesman said. When the carjacker reached for his gun, Brite shot and killed him. (AP) ...*Those luxury car tool boxes sure are well equipped.*

Common Law: David Hoare, 40, had been admitted to a hospital mental ward in Leicester, England, but doctors concluded he was not a threat to others and released him. Hoare, perhaps wanting to prove the doctors wrong, stabbed a stranger, Dianne Moore, 35, to death. Now convicted for killing the woman and confined to a high security mental hospital, Hoare sued the first hospital, contending they should not have let him out. He has been awarded a rumored 30,000 pounds in an out-of-court settlement. (Reuter) ...*America inherited many of its laws from the English. Apparently, they're getting some of our newer legal ideas in exchange.*

Naked Truth: The Vatican has denounced Italian clothing designers for a new "ethically reprehensible and rationally disgusting" trend: having nude or near-nude models in their fashion shows. "The nude, which once was relegated to life behind closed doors, has acquired the function of aiding the fashion world, of being an instrument of publicity to gain attention for their products," complained a spokesman in the official Vatican newspaper. (AP) *...I didn't realize the tourist-attracting statue of David was kept behind "closed" doors. Or the Sistine Chapel. Or....*

Candid Camera: A rare French "spy camera" made in 1882 will be put up for auction in London next month. The camera, which is expected to bring to 35,000 pounds, is hidden in a revolver. It takes a photograph when the trigger is pulled. (Reuter) *...I don't get why the people in your photos are never smiling.*

Voters are Getting Sharper

Governors Fearful Of Cuts

AP headline

Can You Spare a Butt, Gov'ner? George Allen, the governor of Virginia, has been passing out cigarettes. People "should be smoking Virginia cigarettes" if they smoke, he said. "Why smoke North Carolina or Kentucky cigarettes? There are a lot of good cigarettes made in Virginia," he added. Allen doesn't smoke himself, but dips snuff. His brand is made in Tennessee. (AP) *...If his campaign succeeds, more people will die from Virginia cigarettes than from those any other state. That's something any politician can be proud of.*

Shore Patrol: A fight is brewing in the Sydney Harbour National Park in Australia. A beach which was used by nudists for 20 years was closed to the unclothed in 1993 under a new law. Now, New South Wales Environment Minister Pam Allan is attempting to reverse that legislation. However, Mayor Brian Hamer of nearby Manly opposes the reversal, and vows to fight Allen. The stretch in question is visible from the Manly Scenic Walkway. (Australian AP) *...Hamer figures nudists don't pay taxes since they have no pockets.*

Aw, Chute: D'Marc Lee, 23, faced life in prison under California's "three strikes and you're out" law after his conviction for carjacking. While awaiting sentencing, he escaped through a hole he kicked in the wall of his Santa Monica courthouse cell. But he didn't get far: he was unable to get out of the building's ventilation system. Sheriff deputies, who saw him slip through the hole in the wall, evacuated the building and turned off the air conditioning. They searched for him using dogs, motion detectors, and infrared scopes. After more than 24 hours, Lee, who had stripped naked to keep cool, was found and recaptured. He now faces charges of escape. (UPI) ...*The county is appealing its fine for inadequate "Exit" signs in the building.*

Them Too: Reuter recently issued a correction to a story "to correct headline on Dutch item". Rather than the story headlined "Dutch Protestants Unionize to Protect Rights", editors were asked to use the version headed "Dutch Prostitutes Unionize to Protect Rights" instead. (Reuter) ...*Just in time: Hugh Grant was about to change churches.*

Football Fanatics: A Beijing man sentenced to death for murder pled "just wait until after June 14" before executing him because he wanted to see his favorite soccer team, AC Milan, play one last game. The team did win their June 14 match against the Beijing Guoan, but Chinese authorities would not say if they granted the condemned man's wish. Meanwhile, a separate story notes that on July 23, a 29-year-old Shanghai man watched Shandong Taishan, his favorite team, lose 2-1 to team Guoan, but couldn't quite accept the loss. "Jiang, his face shrouded in unhappiness, slowly walked back to his bedroom, locked the door, opened the window and jumped from the fourth floor" to his death, a Shanghai paper reported. (Reuter, 2) ...*"Razors pain you; Rivers are damp; Acids stain you; And drugs cause cramp. Guns aren't lawful; Nooses give; Gas smells awful; You might as well live."* —Dorothy Parker

Detestable Deaths II: A chicken fell down a 60-foot well in Nazlat Imara, 240 miles south of Cairo. A young farmer tried to rescue the bird, but was swept underwater and drowned. His sister, two brothers and two others also drowned, either trying to save the chicken, the farmer, or previous would-be rescuers. All six bodies were recovered. The chicken survived. (Reuter) ...*Not for long, I* *suspect.*

I Told You Not to Bother Me at the Office: Joy Glassman, 60, has been charged with arson for setting as many as 11 fires in the Shasta Trinity National Forest so her firefighter son could get paid more. "She just did it on her own, figuring she was helping him," noted Mark Reina, an investigator for the California Forestry Department, adding that they do not believe her son knew about her activities. Glassman faces 20 years in prison. Her son has resigned his job. (AP) ...*So back to his old job, replacing the street signs that keep disappearing from his neighborhood.*

Say It Ain't So: On Thursday, the Oxford University Press will publish the "Plain English Guide", a new book on grammar which puts to rest some old rules. "If you think a sentence will be more emphatic, clear or rhythmical, split your infinitive," the guide counsels. But to ruthlessly split infinitives might be considered an abomination by some English teachers. Author Martin Cutts, who is also the research director of the Plain Language Commission, adds it's also OK to start sentences with "but". "Jane Austen begins sentences with 'but' on almost every page, and occasionally uses 'and' in the same position," Cutts notes. And so onward goes the language. (Reuter) ...*So a traditionalist isn't always an easy thing to continue being one of.*

We're Not Amused, We're Sort-of British: Hong Kong's High Court Justice Jim Findlay has denounced a ruling by the Obscene Articles Tribunal that a photograph of Michelangelo's masterpiece marble statue "David" was obscene. The ruling stated that the photo of the "wholly naked male person with his penis fully exposed was out of order," and that the newspaper which published it should be fined $25,641 and the editor should spend a year in jail. Judge Findlay noted the decision was "out of order", "totally incomprehensible", and would make Hong Kong the "laughing stock of the world." (UPI) ...*The members of the Tribunal should be fined $25,641 and sentenced to a year in jail.*

What Are the Odds?
Gambling Ship May Have Sunk
AP headline

You Heard Me: Students learning English in the Puttalam district of Sri Lanka were presented with a skills test recently. Questions on the test included "Why not do you like one this are?", "How about this are sir? Will I can give it to you for 300 rupies.", and "You want to apply for a soholarship to a college in England. Complele this application from." (Reuter) *...If you think that's bad, wait until you see what the official answers were.*

Judicial Relief: The attorneys general of New York and Pennsylvania are pushing for federal legislation to stop frivolous and malicious lawsuits by state prisoners. One New York inmate sued because the prison made him use white towels — he preferred beige. A Pennsylvania inmate filed a lawsuit stating that he owned all mineral rights in Pennsylvania and Texas, and thus was demanding $700 trillion for all of "his" oil that had been taken from the ground without his permission. Another, Ronald McDonald, sued because he was removed from a work-release program when it was discovered that — yes — he was stealing hamburgers. (UPI) *...Plus he wants compensation because he claims the McDonalds "Hamburglar" character was based on him.*

Fine for Feeding: Moskovsky Komsomolets, a Russian newspaper, reports that the Moscow Zoo will levy a fine equivalent to $125 — about 10 months' pay for an entry-level worker — on people who feed the animals. "Oddly enough," the paper notes, "those trying to get into the cage with the beasts (which in certain cases would amount to feeding them) will face a fine only a tenth the size." (Reuter) *...Naturally: such entertainment attracts more visitors.*

I'll See You in Court: In 1993, a blind man learning how to work with a seeing-eye dog in a mall in Tampa, Fla., encountered the Rev. William E. Christian and his wife, Carolyn. The dog tried to steer him around the couple, but, apparently confused, the man stepped on Carolyn's foot, breaking her toe. Witnesses said Mrs. Christian made no attempt to move out of the way, but that didn't stop her from suing the guide dog school for $80,000 for medical bills, pain, suffering, humiliation and disability. Rev. Christian also sued for $80,000 for loss of his wife's "care, comfort and consortium." But when news of the lawsuit hit local newspapers and radio talk shows, mounting public outrage prompted the lawyer who filed the suit to withdraw it, and he says his firm will donate $1000 to the school. (AP) ...*There's nothing like the light of day to make the roaches run and hide.*

Youth Hostel: For the second year in a row, a Venezuela children's team in the U.S. for a baseball tournament is staying at the Seminole Health Club in Davie, Fla. — a nudist resort. "Seen it before," noted one boy when asked what he thought. One 12-year-old girl was asked what she saw. "Everything. In detail," she said. Are their parents worried? "I was a little concerned last year," said one mother who was chaperoning the kids. "But everyone here is really nice, and no one is *doing* anything." Indeed, the club's owner said, "the kids don't make a big deal out of it." (AP) ...*Kids never enjoy the scenes of nature when on vacation.*

On the Plus Side: Stalwart Assurance of London is offering a special deal to some customers. Annuity buyers who attest that they have smoked for at least 10 years will receive a higher annuity payment since, statistically, they will surely die sooner — though the buyers are not required to continue smoking. "It's not intended to be something which is an inducement or encouragement to smoke," said a Stalwart spokesman. "We are just reflecting the fact that the health damage has been done." The company is now looking into similar policies for obese people, and perhaps those with high cholesterol. (Reuter) ...*Suicidal obese smoking hypertensive heroin addicts should form a single line at Window A.*

You're Fired: In the wake of continued high-publicity shootings around the country, the U.S. Postal Service's Board of Governors has decided that any postal employee found in possession of a gun at work will be summarily dismissed. "No ifs, ands or buts," Postmaster General Marvin Runyon said. "Employees everywhere — in every company — should come to work without having to worry," he said. (AP) ...*Let's see: life in prison doesn't deter them, but the thought of losing a high stress job will. Got it.*

Break a Leg: Tenor Fabio Armiliato, on stage during a performance of "Tosca" in Macerata, Italy, was particularly startled when the guns went off in the firing squad scene. As the audience applauded, Armiliato yelled "They really shot at me!" and grabbed his foot. "At first I thought it was a director's trick, but it was real blood, and the tenor was crying out in pain," said lead actress Raina Kabaivanska. Police are investigating the incident. (AP) ...*Ah, but how did she know it was real blood, and that he wasn't just acting? Don't leave town, Miss Kabaivanska.*

Pineapple Juice

Drunk Soldiers Fooling with a Grenade are Blown to Bits

Reuter headline

You Have Been Replaced: The migration of people from Thailand's coconut plantations to better-paying jobs in the city has left a shortage of workers to climb the trees to harvest the crop. Pigtail monkeys have been trained to take their place. A recent competition showed that a monkey can climb a tree, select eight ripe nuts, pick them, and drop them to the ground in just 34 seconds. It has been estimated that 1200 monkeys now work in southern Thailand's coconut plantations. (Reuter) ...*However, the rumor that Bill Gates has 1200 monkeys working at 1200 terminals to produce "Windows 96" is just that: a rumor.*

Taste Test: In the recent waterlogged movie "Waterworld", Kevin Costner's character drinks his own urine. Nothing new, "urotherapy" followers claim. The practice is centuries old and can help cure everything from TB to jet lag. But lately, Newsweek notes, it has become somewhat of a "gee whiz" fad in the U.S. and Britain. Doctors argue that "if the body is trying to eliminate something from the system, that would be a sign that it's not a good idea to ingest it." Nonsense, says Vedanta Saraswati, a London yoga teacher: "Westerners in general are awfully funny about things that come out of orifices." (Newsweek) *...Hey, pal: be careful not to spit when you talk.*

Please Try Again: The Oakfield Football Club on the Isle of Wight, England, failed to get a grant from Britain's National Lottery to build a new 75,000-pound sports hall. Thinking that perhaps another artistic endeavor might be looked on more favorably, the team changed its name to the Oakfield Operatic Society and is apparently asking for 75,000 pounds to build a new opera house. The team will continue to play soccer, but "we'll give the singing a go. Who knows, we may find a budding Pavarotti among our ranks," the team's manager said. (Reuter) *...You can get one hell of a vibrato by whacking a guy in the head with the ball.*

And Hurry! Oklahoma prison inmate Robert Brecheen was found in his cell, overdosed on sedatives, at 9:00 p.m. Officials rushed the convicted murderer to the hospital to be revived, and returned him to the prison just two hours late for his midnight execution by lethal injection. "Certainly, there's irony" in the case, said Oklahoma Corrections Department director Larry Fields, but, a spokeswoman for the state attorney general added, the U.S. Supreme Court has ruled that a condemned prisoner "has to be aware of his execution and he has to know why he is being executed." Guards and defense attorneys — the last to visit Brecheen — are being questioned to determine where the inmate got the drugs. (AP) *...Now I lay me down to sleep. If I should die before I wake, several laws I'm sure to break.*

Beam Him Aboard: Ian Crawford, an astronomer at London's University College, recently published a paper which argues that the laws of physics allow the kinds of things seen in "Star Trek" — faster-than-light transit through space wormholes or by the use of warp drives. "The proofs are complex and mathematical, but more and more astrophysicists are satisfied that in theory it is possible," he says. But Simon Mitton, spokesman for the British Astronomical Society, said people should be skeptical: "It is quite important to realize that when learned societies publish a paper of any sort, the publication of the paper does not imply the collective endorsement of the entire society," he sniffed. (Reuter) *...Mr. Scott: set your phaser on fry and burn that guy to the ground.*

Call of the Wild: Stuck in the city? Can't drag yourself off the couch to visit nature? Call Paris's Association for the Protection of Wild Animals and Natural Inheritance hotline. For about 45 cents per minute, you can hear animals threatened by extinction: howling wolves, songs of the whales, and bleating Alpine sheep, among others. The hotline allows callers to "to listen to nature as if you were there," the Association said. (AP) *...This suggests maybe they should have a tape of a bleating Parisian.*

Post No Bills: In "a small step for the people behind the project but a giant leap for modern marketing," the Gazolin&S advertising agency in Sweden is taking bids from companies wanting to advertise on the side of a rocket loaded with scientific payloads being launched by the European Space Agency. The minimum bid: $1 million. For this, the advertiser will also "get exclusive footage of their own advertising in space," Gazolin&S executive vice-president Robert Bryhn said. It's a good thing: the ad will only be visible for about 10 seconds by viewers on the ground. The funds will help offset the cost of future research. (Reuter) *...That's nothing new: advertisers are used to their campaigns going up in smoke.*

Duh

TV Talk Shows a Danger
to Mental Health

UPI headline

This Just In: The front page of the Aspen (Colo.) Daily News told the whole story. A local woman, it reported, "rampaged through local singles bars Wednesday night, leaving a string of wasted males in her wake." Indeed, "no less than 37 men aged 13 to 78 were taken to local hospitals. Their injuries included everything from severe bleeding due from hickies on their necks to sexual exhaustion." But the reporter who wrote the story created it as a joke for his girlfriend, and never intended for the file to get into the paper's typesetting system — let alone the front page. Locals were far from outraged: some bought extra copies, and "people are asking us to run this once a week," the news editor said. (AP) *...Are they going to punish the reporter, or promote him?*

This Won't Hurt a Bit: Researchers at the Anuradhapura Hospital in Sri Lanka have come up with a new anti-venin for victims of the Russell's viper, one of many poisonous snakes in the region. But to win government approval, they must test the new potion on at least 75 bite victims by the end of October, and they're behind schedule. "We are desperately in need of victims," one of the doctors in the study said. "The victims don't have to be Sri Lankan. Anyone is welcome." (Reuter) *...Everyone needs to pitch in: if you are bitten, book a flight immediately.*

This Won't Hurt a Bit II: E.J. Mallory, an American Army dentist assigned to occupied Japan after World War II, was asked to make a set of dentures for Gen. Hideki Tojo, who was imprisoned awaiting trial for war crimes. Mallory, knowing who the dentures were for, inscribed a Morse code message onto the false teeth of the man who approved the surprise attack on Hawaii that brought the U.S. into the war: "Remember Pearl Harbor". Mallory said recently the gag "wasn't anything done in anger. It's just that not many people had the chance to get those words into his mouth." A ham radio operator, Mallory used code instead of block letters to keep the message hidden. But the secret leaked out within weeks, and Mallory had to wake Tojo in the middle of the night to remove the phrase. The next morning, when an officer demanded to know "Is there any truth in this report that 'Remember Pearl Harbor' is inscribed in the dentures?", Mallory was able to truthfully answer, "No Sir!" (AP) *...He took the words right out* *of my mouth.*

There's a Term for That: In 1990, California voters approved a measure to limit the terms of state politicians — after three two-year terms (Assembly) or two four-year terms (Senate), legislators must either quit or run for other offices. Due to the law, 46 legislators cannot run in the next election. But that hasn't stopped them from taking campaign contributions: the 46 have raised average campaign chests of $106,329 each — including a mighty $1.03 million by Assembly speaker Willie Brown — compared to an average of $91,565 each for legislators that *can* run again. The law allows contributions to be diverted to races for other offices, or they can be donated to other candidates. (AP) *...When you mix politicians and cash, there's always a loophole.*

Not in My Backyard: A community in southwest Ireland doesn't want a proposed crematorium to be installed at a local church. They say the facility would be unfriendly to the environment, and would damage the good name of the area. The community is known as Ovens. (Reuter) *...Sure, they think this is a half-baked idea, but with some promotion it could become the toast of the town.*

Beyond a Reasonable Doubt: Kristine Eagle, a Stockton, Calif., public defender representing David Huffman in his trial for murder, had her defense ideas go out the door when her client took the stand. "I wanted someone I can have control over. I wanted to ruin someone else's day," Huffman said, admitting his guilt from the stand. Upon hearing his testimony, Eagle fainted and fell to the courtroom floor. (AP) *...These days, just the very idea of a person taking responsibility for his own actions is enough to completely overwhelm some people.*

Judicial Restraint: London Judge John Wroath was getting ready for court when he discovered his horsehair wig and robe were missing. His 30-year-old son, a singer in the rock band "Wayward Sons", had borrowed them for use on stage. "If I ever find him near them again, he will feel the full force of my law," the judge decreed. (Reuter) *...Maybe it could be worse: what does your wife do, sir?*

Charge It: Cindy Penka called her husband Thomas at the electronics store where he works to tell him that she had just been robbed of her purse. As they discussed canceling her credit cards, a store clerk signaled Thomas that someone had just handed him one of Cindy's credit cards for a purchase. Thomas told Cindy he had to go, then called police. The clerk was able to stall long enough for police to arrive and arrest two men on larceny and forgery charges. (AP) *...Just their rotten luck: the clerk knew Cindy didn't have a moustache.*

Talent Day at the Farm
Couple Produces Organic Milk
AP headline

Final Notice: A collection agency hired to collect a $2000 balance on Albert and Marianne Driscol's Visa credit card went just a bit too far, a Texas court ruled. The agency, Mrs. Driscol said, harassed her at work and in the middle of the night, calling her every few minutes. After several months came the final straw: a threat to "put a contract out" on Mrs. Driscol's life, she said, followed by a bomb threat at her office. A jury awarded the Driscols $2 million in actual damages plus $9 million in punitive damages. The collection agency is already out of business, so Household Credit Services, Inc., who hired the agency but never bothered to respond to the lawsuit, has been ordered to pay the award. (AP) *...And hurry up, before they hire an experienced collector to squeeze it out of you.*

Spell Check: Susan Leybourne is on a campaign to show that pagans aren't bad people — they just suffer from bad publicity. "People think we dance around fires naked all the time," she says, "but it's too cold in Britain" for that. Priestess Leybourne, one of 12 chaplains at Leeds University, is the first pagan ever to become a university chaplain in England. Being a witch isn't easy in a modern world, Leybourne says. "Usually the way to send spells off into the astral world is to burn them or put them into running water like a stream," she says. But as a child learning about her religion, "I didn't have a stream, so I had to flush them down the toilet." (Reuter) ...*At least someone is finally doing something about the alligators in the sewers.*

Ready, Set, Go to Jail: Using careful planning to cut out wasted time, Patrick Mitchell and his "Stopwatch Gang" may be the U.S.'s most successful bank robbers. At least, until now. Never satisfied with small takes in more than 100 robberies since 1980, Mitchell looked for hauls of "over $100,000, and if we thought it would be less, we didn't go." Recently, Mitchell spent weeks preparing for a robbery in Southaven, Tenn. "This bank my sister could have robbed," he said. "It was an easy, easy bank. There was nothing to it." To throw police off before going in, Mitchell phoned in a bomb threat to city hall — but the police chief knew that trick. "There's only nine banks in the whole town and the police chief sent a police car to every one of them," Mitchell said. They were in and out of the bank in 45 seconds with their loot, but the police were outside waiting. (AP) ...*Never underestimate small town cops. They have the time to think.*

I Can Dig It: It's expensive to die in Bucharest. A local newspaper advises readers to "bring your own gravediggers and save money." Fees for digging a burial plot can easily reach 70,000 lei (US$35) — more than many Romanians can afford. But one city official denied people can bring their own shovels. "We don't let amateurs dig graves in our cemeteries," he sniffed. (Reuter) ...*However, we will rent you one of our approved, professional shovels for just 30,000 lei.*

Campus Digs: To attract and keep students, colleges are starting to add all the comforts of home — and more — to their dorms. "For a lot of students, the academic program is not their top priority," admits the housing director at San Antonio's University of Texas. Purdue has hired a full-time marketing representative to show students their call waiting and in-room movies so they know "how good they really do have it," said the Indiana university's residence hall director. "Students come to school expecting their own room, TV and an Internet hookup," agrees the residential director of Illinois State University. Students there can also order room service using their fax machines. (AP) ...*Why, yes,* **have** *been thinking about grad school lately. How did you know?*

Stuff It: Progress isn't always welcome. As the campaign to replace the paper dollar bill with a coin gains momentum in the U.S., one's thoughts invariably turn to those adversely affected. Like strippers. The long-honored tradition of slipping a buck in a G-string may finally be over. "All that weight! We wouldn't be able to carry it if we got, like, 20 singles in coins," said one dancer, considering the horror. "When you tip the girl a dollar, there is a brief bond there, or an imagined bond between the girl and the guy. To just drop a dollar coin into a cup, it's just not the same," lamented one industry observer. (Washington Post) ...*Time to bring the $2 bill back into general circulation — surely the dancers need a raise by now.*

All Right, Pull Over: A woman has been banished from Disneyland for one month for speeding in the park. In her wheelchair. A spokesman said it was the third time Katrina Laurent had been stopped for excessive speed — about 4.5 mph — and another guest complained about being bumped. "The only time I've ever hit someone is if they jump suddenly in front of me," said Laurent, who visits the park almost daily under a $199 annual pass. (AP) ...*No matter where in the park you are, "Big Mouse" is watching you.*

I'm Not a Fugitive, But I Play One on TV: Twelve convicts escaped from the Vridsloeselille state jail in Copenhagen when a bulldozer crashed through the security perimeter. A Danish television crew was there in time to tape the event, leading to charges of complicity. The crew admitted to receiving a tip that a "happening" would take place, but "we had no idea it would be a jailbreak. If we had known, we would naturally have informed the police," they said. Nine of the escapees remain at large. (Reuter) ...*A snitch in time frees nine.*

Services to be Held from 2:00 to 2:05
Reading Wiz Evelyn Wood Dies
AP headline

I'm So Depressed: About five percent of people on the anti-depressant drug clomipramine have noticed an interesting side effect: when they yawn, they have an orgasm. While a more common side effect of the drug is a reduction in sexual desire, "one woman, better after being depressed for three months, wanted to keep taking the tablets" so she could continue enjoying the side effect, a report in the journal New Scientist noted. Some can produce the result by purposefully yawning, but others "would presumably actively seek out the most boring person they could find at parties," the journal said. (Reuter) *...What a terrible TV show! Was it good for you, too?*

Land Shark: For 20 years, the Blackwater River State Forest, north of Pensacola, Fla., has been known as a place where hunting dogs disappear. One of the most recent, Flojo, was a $5,000 Walker fox-hunting hound. Armed with a direction-finding device to detect a transmitter on the dog's collar, Rufus Godwin found his dog. "When we walked up to this hole, just all of a sudden the [radio locator] boxes went to beeping out of sight," Godwin said. During the fight to capture the 11-foot, 50-year-old alligator hiding in the hole, the monster spit up Flojo's collar. Several other collars were found in the belly of the beast, including one from a dog that disappeared 14 years ago. The walking handbag was near a popular swimming hole. "As long as we kept carrying him $5,000 dogs, he was eating good," Godwin said, and thus didn't need to snack on children swimming nearby. (AP) *...If hunters hadn't been shooting nearby, those children could have been in real danger.*

Pass the Vinegar: "Our goal is to offer women an opportunity to achieve a satisfactory image in the safest possible way," said LipoMatrix Inc. president Terry Knapp, launching a new breast implant filled not with silicone, but salad oil. "It's natural, safe and secure." Looking to relive the glory days when "225 million [sic] breast implants were sold" in the U.S. in one year (1990), the company thinks the next big market is Asia. "We anticipate [the current $250 million worldwide market] is going to increase substantially," Knapp said. (Reuter) ... *Those figures sound artificially inflated.*

Now See Here: Gary Gunderson, 43, convicted of embezzlement and grand theft, told the judge in his sentencing hearing that his eyesight was so poor, he didn't realize how much government property he had stolen while on the job with the Forest Service. Forest Service officials said that "truckloads" of goods, including furniture and a generator, were found on Gunderson's northern California property. Judge William Polley saw the problem clearly, and sentenced Gunderson to prison and probation. (AP) *...If he couldn't see, how did he drive the truckloads home?*

Huh? Where? II: The American Life League, a Virginia-based anti-abortion group, claims that many of Disney's animated children's features contain subliminal sexual imagery. The latest, they charge, is in "The Lion King", where a cloud of dust over Simba spells out the word "sex". In "The Little Mermaid", a minister shows "obvious sexual arousal", while "Aladdin" contains a voice which whispers "good teenagers, take off your clothes." A Disney spokesman says the claims are "ridiculous". (Reuter) *...Ah! But "ridiculous" anagrams to "curious lid", and "spokesman" is "keno spasm" (or, worse, "Kemp? No ass"), and "Disney" itself unscrambles to "Dye Sin"! Explain* **that,** *fast-talker!*

Mystery Meat: John Darmstadt, a University of Virginia food service official, was so upset over a campus newspaper review of the food served in his facility that he hid 4,000 of the 6,000 copies of the paper that were printed. "This culinary comedy of errors will serve as the butt of many jokes between you and your cohorts for years to come," the review said, under the headline "Beware of Inedible Horrors Lurking in University's Dining Halls". Darmstadt, who insists his food is "very, very good," apologized and returned the papers. (AP) *...Of course he did. He was caught.*

Woof: As the O.J. Simpson case drags on, concern is mounting over whether the sequestered jurors can stand it to the end. "I've got a jury going nuts," Judge Lance Ito told the attorneys in the case. To help stem boredom, several outings for the jurors have been made, but a boat trip to the offshore Catalina Island resort area didn't help the panel's mood: choppy waters led to seasickness. "The jury, I'm told, are not happy campers. Apparently they came back from Catalina barking at the seals," Ito said. (AP) *...This may end up being the first case of "not guilty by reason of the jury's insanity".*

Hurry, They're Going Fast
Study: Few Jobs From NAFTA
AP headline

Report: No New Jobs From NAFTA
AP headline, the next day

Call Me Pinocchio: Faced with rapidly stiffening opposition, an AIDS awareness advertisement has been pulled from Brazilian television just days after it started. The ad, which features a man in a bar talking with his penis, known as Braulio, promotes the use of condoms. "If you come out you're going to have to wear a condom," the man tells his pants. "OK, you win," the unseen Braulio responds, "but get the condom quickly because there's a gorgeous woman staring at me." Much of the opposition to the ad came from people named Braulio. The name was chosen after a survey found it a common Brazilian nickname for the male organ. Anastacio, Bimbo ("too childish"), Mauro, Petronio ("too long"), Oscar and Tonhao, were also considered. Brazil's health minister Adib Jatene defended the $5 million ad campaign as "daring and aggressive", and necessary to help combat the fact that Brazil has the greatest incidence of AIDS in Latin America. He says the ads will reappear after a new nickname is chosen. (Reuter, AP) *...Be macho, Minister Jatene: change his name to "Adib".*

Desperate Criminal: Nancy Stein brought William, her four-year-old grandson, to New York's Central Park for an outing when the lad announced "I have to go." Right now, that is. With no toilet facilities nearby, William made use of a nearby bush. But even before he was finished, two Parks Commission security guards ticketed Stein for the "deposit of a noxious liquid" — complete with a $50 fine. "I guess I was incredulous. I guess I was in shock," Stein recalled. She appealed the fine through several city departments, but it wasn't until the case hit the newspapers that the park commissioner stepped in and dismissed the ticket. "It was a rookie officer" who "acted in haste," the commissioner explained. (AP) *...So did William, but he had a good excuse.*

Puffed Rice: A new wedding dress was unveiled at a bridal fair in England last week, a white one designed for pregnant brides. "Being unmarried and pregnant is no longer a taboo," says designer Jennie Andrews. "It is only fair that pregnant brides should have a beautiful dress. After all, they are blooming." The gown, which will retail for about $775, is the first traditional maternity wedding dress on the market, Andrews said. (Reuter) *...It's a fine idea, but advertising "traditional" and "maternity wedding dress" together seems like such a Calvin Klein thing to do.*

Reboot: A 19-year-old University of Delaware student fell three stories from his dorm room balcony after losing his balance while sitting on the rail, leaving him in serious condition. Just an hour earlier, in an apparently unrelated incident, another 19-year-old student was having trouble with his computer in his dorm room. He "got up and ran around the room in a pique of anger," a witness said, and then slammed his fist into his window. Not only did that break the window, but the student, apparently surprised that the glass didn't hold his weight, lost his balance and fell through—13 stories to his death. (AP) *...You can save your life if you repeat after me: It's just a computer, and I have a backup. It's just a computer, and....*

It's Clever, But is it Art? State Farm Fire and Casualty wants its money back. The insurer sold a policy to Lucio Ambroselli to cover several expensive works of art, including two paintings, allowing photographs of the paintings to be submitted as proof of ownership. Three weeks later, Ambroselli reported the artwork stolen and collected $410,000 in damages. The problem? State Farm says their investigations show the photographs were taken in the Vatican Art Museum, where the paintings have hung for centuries, and not in Ambroselli's California home — where the other artworks were found in a police search. Ambroselli has been arrested and faces five years in prison and a $250,000 fine. (AP) *...Who knew insurance investigators could afford to vacation in Europe?*

One or the Other: When a resolution passed at the International Institute of Communications' conference in Osaka, Japan, declaring that advances in telecommunications would usher in an era of "heaven on Earth", American lawyer Delbert Smith had something to say. "Hell is a loss of privacy, and nothing brings us closer to hell than telecommunications technology," he said. But "the Cold War was won not by weapons but by international broadcasters using technology to break jamming signals," argued another delegate. "Heaven (in Eastern Europe) was created not by the sword but by the word." Smith won the day, however: the resolution was overturned. (Reuter) *...Of course he won. American lawyers are renowned experts in the creation of hell.*

Thirsty: Samuel Hernandez spent five years in pain after surgery, going to doctor after doctor to find out why. Finally, a Miami doctor x-rayed him and found the cause: the surgeon in the original 1988 operation left a towel inside him. It has now been removed, and Hernandez is trying to sue the doctor and hospital, despite the expiration of a four-year statute of limitations. (AP) *...Worse, they charged him $288 for that towel.*

Hungry: A survey by the British magazine Men's Health found that British men fantasize about having sex 2,555 times a year — about seven times per day. "Sexual fantasy improves the quality of your actual sex life," the magazine said. Further, "sexual fantasies occur most often in men who enjoy the greatest sexual satisfaction." Their advice, then? "Dream on." (Reuter) ...*If they think they can handle sex seven times a day, they **are** dreaming.*

Exhibit A: The warden of the new Allegheny County Jail in Pittsburgh has a problem: prisoners are stripping and exposing themselves through their windows, which face downtown streets. Some inmates flash their girlfriends, who loiter on the street to see their locked up loved ones, but there are also bus stops in front of the jail. "I don't want the general public harassed," the warden says, adding he finds the inmates' behavior "amusing". He plans to have the glass sandblasted to make the windows opaque. But it's not just a public problem: cells on the women's side of the holding facility face the men's side, and the inmates are exposing themselves to each other, too. (UPI) ...*Nothing to get excited about. I'm sure it's just a flash in the pen.*

Boing!

23-foot-long Python Squeezes Rubber Worker

Reuter headline

Fax Me When You Get There: Apparently tired of inefficient seances and Oujia boards, the dead have turned to faxes and (yes!) electronic mail to communicate with the living, says Pat Kubis, a retired Orange County (Calif.) teacher, and Mark Macy, who have written a book on the subject. The dead have described heaven as a planet in the spiral galaxy NGC4866, and is a wonderful place — exactly "what you believe it is," they say. Yes, but e-mail from heaven? A spokeswoman from America Online says she's never heard of it, but it would be OK with them — though any dead people using the service "would have to have a living checking account or credit card" to pay for their online time. (L.A. Times) ...*The American Express Card: Don't Leave This Astral Plane Without It.*

Call Me if You Need Me: Donna Graybeal's telephone rang every 90 minutes. No one was ever there. "It drives you absolutely out of your mind," she said. "I thought, talk dirty to me. Do something!" — but they never did. The Billerica, Mass., woman put up with the problem for about six months, or about 2700 calls, before making a call of her own to police. The problem was quickly traced to an oil tank in the basement of the James family in Potomac, Md. The tank had been equipped with a telephone dialer in a test eight years ago to alert the oil company when it was empty, and the family had stopped using the tank. Graybeal ended up with the oil company's telephone number, and the calls. (Washington Post) ...*Ah, but six months ago, Donna's aunt Gertrude died and was buried in Maryland. Coincidence? You be the judge.*

Power Play: Military sites in Russia have had their electricity cut off 16 times since 1992 for non-payment. Most recently, a nuclear submarine base had its power cut off after its bill got up to $4.5 million. The commander was so incensed that he sent troops to force the restoration of power at gunpoint. Power company officials have protested, noting "the fact that military people can come to our premises and dictate their terms at gunpoint causes great ...anxiety." (AP) ...*You mean, that's something new?*

Revolutionary Wear: A Wal-Mart store in Miramar, Fla., has pulled a T-shirt from its shelves, apologizing that it was "offensive" and, a headquarters spokeswoman said, because it "goes against Wal-Mart's family values," it would not be available in any Wal-Mart. The subversive T-shirt, sponsored by Women are Wonderful Inc., showed a female cartoon character saying "Someday a woman will be president". (AP) ...*Not if Wal-Mart's "family values" have anything to say about it.*

If You Say So: The World Bank, apparently trying to prove that statistics can be bent to show anything, has determined that the United States is far from the richest country on Earth. In fact, it is number 12, behind Australia, Canada, Luxembourg, Switzerland, Japan, Sweden, Iceland, Qatar, the United Arab Emirates and Denmark (number 11 was not specified). Their model "challenges conventional thinking" and "expands the concept of wealth beyond money and investments" by assigning values to natural resources, capital resources, productivity and education while ignoring a country's actual economic output, a World Bank spokesman said. (Reuter) *...We must qualify for some sort of foreign aid, then, eh?*

See Me After Class: Frankfort, Ky., high school Spanish teacher Fran Cook breathed a sigh of relief at the end of last school year: she looked forward to being rid of a problem student. However, Andy Bray, 18, apparently left instructions with friends on how to effectively disrupt Cook's classes. School administrators only gave Bray a 40-minute detention, so Cook took matters to a higher authority: she sued Bray, charging terrorism. A jury found Bray "clearly exceeded the bounds of common decency" and awarded Cook $8,700 for her emotional distress and medical bills, plus $25,000 in punitive damages and a restraining order. Cook has now retired, ending her 25-year career, and will use her court award to help other teachers in similar situations. (AP) *...How about making the parents write "We will control our children" on the blackboard 200 times?*

Animal Kingdom: Birdwatchers flocked from all over England to see a rare red-necked phalarope on a stopover during its migration from Scotland to Africa. As it swam in a reservoir in Leicestershire, the birders watched something "like a scene from 'Jaws'," one witness said. "One second the bird was swimming, the next there was a snap and a splash and it vanished." A four-foot pike had swallowed the bird in one bite, leaving only a few floating feathers. (Reuter) *...Maybe that's nature's way of saying it doesn't want big audiences.*

First Tests Near Chernobyl
Plants that Glow in Dark Could Help Farmers
Reuter headline

Leveled: The world headquarters of the Flat Earth Society, which is also the home of its president, Charles Johnson, burned down this week. In addition to personal belongings, all of the Society's records were lost, including membership information. Johnson denies that the Society is anti-social. "We're not enemies of America, but we don't believe the hoax that the world is a globe," he says. "If you like the spinning ball, stay with it." (LA Daily News) ...*They're sure to get letters of sympathy from all around the world.*

Uh Oh: The British journal Nature has published a "map" of half of the 80,000 DNA sequences of the human cell. The 379-page catalog contains the complete sequences for several genes. (AP) ...*Great: as soon as part 2 comes out, some kid is going to go and build one.*

Jailhouse Sweet Jailhouse: A month ago [*see* "I'm Not a Fugitive, But I Play One on TV", *page 33*], a dozen inmates in a Danish prison escaped when a bulldozer cut through the security perimeter. But one of the escapees, Kim Steven Kyed, 27, apparently didn't enjoy life on the outside: he recently showed up at the prison gates and asked to be let back in. At the time of the breakout, a number of inmates were enjoying an outdoor steak picnic, and didn't even bother to attempt escaping. (Reuter) ...*He left before dessert, and just couldn't get it out of his mind.*

No Way O.J.: Bill Ritchie, a Concord, N.H., trademark lawyer, was outraged to learn that O.J. Simpson's attorneys had filed trademark applications to register the terms "O.J." and "Juice" for his exclusive use or licensing for 120 products. Trademark law does not allow the registration of marks that are "immoral" or "scandalous". Ritchie thinks he has a case: "I think capitalizing on his name is scandalous," he said. "It's like 'Jeffrey Dahmer Soup'." (AP) ...*Nah, no one would go that far. That would be as horrendous as, say, a Charles Manson record album!*

Trademarks II: A New York federal judge has ruled that a character in a new "Muppets" movie in production can keep its name, Spa'am, despite the objections of Hormel Foods Corp., the makers of SPAM, the forever-popular mystery meat in a can.

Judge Kimba Wood said the movie-going public is unlikely to confuse the character, a stuffed toy puppet, with Hormel's product. Hormel plans to appeal. (AP) ...*They have a point: leave SPAM out for a day or two, and it does get furry, move by itself, and talk.*

Ssssenssssational: Mohd Yusof wants to prove snakes aren't so bad — and break a record set by his uncle. To do this, the Singapore snake charmer plans to spend two weeks in a cage with 300 poisonous snakes at the Kuala Lumpur Zoo; in 1987, his uncle spent just 10 days with only 200 snakes. The only catch: Yusof has to provide his own snakes. "I am looking for sponsors to buy more snakes," he said. "So far I have five." (Reuter) ...*Apparently his uncle isn't interested in loaning any of his.*

Animal Farm: Harder times for farmers, coupled with families that have never known more than the urban landscapes they grew up in, have combined into a new tourist attraction: working farms. "She gave birth in front of 50 to 60 people," beams hog farmer Fred Sepe, pointing out a sow during a tour on his farm outside New York City. "She performed very well." And the tourists don't take much effort to entertain: "We found that a lot of people want to just hang around," Sepe said. (AP) ...*And best of all, visitors can take a piece of the attraction back home for their freezer.*

Tastes Like Chicken: Ornithologists studying the birds of Papua New Guinea's rainforests think the variable pitohui may be poisonous, just like its cousin, the hooded pitohui. "When I licked the feathers I felt my mouth tingle and go numb," said Phil Gregory, who publishes an ornithology journal when not taste-testing fauna. But "we need to net a couple of these birds and send them for testing before we can confirm this." (Reuter) ...*If you had left some of the first one, maybe we'd know by now.*

Smelled Fishy: Heterodoxy, a journal published by the Los Angeles-based Center for the Study of Popular Culture which "skewers and ridicules the politically correct," recently published a story about a man lost in the mountains of New York who survived only by eating squirrels cooked by focusing the sun's rays with his eyeglasses. The joke? That he was being prosecuted by animal rights activists for eating too many squirrels. The punch line? Many legitimate media outlets repeated the story as fact, including Paul Harvey News and ABC's "This Week with David Brinkley". CSPC spokesman John Herr noted most readers realized the satire by the fourth paragraph, but the fact that many news outlets [not including *This is True,* of course] ran the story proved their point: "We've gotten so out of control," he says. (AP) ... *They had to make something up: no one believes the true stories because they're too outlandish.*

Me First: When both paid and volunteer firefighters from the Prince George's County (Md.) fire department arrived at a house fire at the same time, an argument erupted as to which group would get to carry the first hose. Police had to intervene to break up the fight. Two paid firefighters and six volunteers have been suspended. (AP) ...*If the police hadn't broken up the fight, the issue would have been decided already.*

Passing Bills
Cash Found In Man's Stomach
AP headline

Tippler Gore: Vice President Al Gore's daughter, Sarah, 16, has been cited by police for drinking beer in public. Her mother has spoken extensively in the past about the dangers of underage drinking. (AP) ...*Don't worry — she swears she didn't swallow.*

Commuting with Nature: A number of British readers of the journal New Scientist believe that pigeons travel around London by train. One wrote to the journal to assert that the birds have figured out that "travel by Tube saves their wings." Another said she saw two pigeons getting on a train at Aldgate, then "alighting with purpose" at Tower Hill. "How did they know the platform for Tower Hill was the same side of the carriage as that for Aldgate?" she wrote. (Reuter) ...*Easy: they just queued up with everyone else.*

Bird News II: Buckingham Palace confirmed reports that Queen Elizabeth was hit by a bird. Attending a grouse shoot in Scotland last month, "a shot bird spiraled from the sky on a misty morning and brushed off the queen's shoulder," a Palace spokesman said. The kamikaze Celt hit her hard enough to cause a bruise. "A famous grouse perhaps it may become, but not one that will alter the course of history," the spokesman added. (AP) ...*No, but it was a course at dinner.*

Home Run: Richard Murphy collected about 250 baseballs that splashed into his pool, hit his roof, or went through his windows — all from a Little League baseball diamond that backs up to his house in Henderson, Nev. "What else does it take to end this madness? Someone dying from a head injury?" he asked. Apparently, it takes more than what he did: he stole the bases, police say, taking them from the field so people couldn't play anymore. He has been arrested and charged with larceny. (AP) ...*That's double jeopardy — he's already been charged with an error.*

Fire in the Hole: A gang of thieves tried to break into a fireworks factory in Kent, England — with a blowtorch. The resulting explosion destroyed the factory and set the gang's van on fire. Police have dubbed the group "The Hole in the Ground Gang". (Reuter) ...*They'll be arrested as soon as they get back to Earth.*

Falling Stars: "Many people see this as an appropriate way to express their interest in space," notes Charles Chafer. The vice president of Celestis, Inc., was speaking of a plan to launch "a symbolic portion" of a cremated person's ashes into orbit in a small capsule for $4,800. A similar plan failed to fly in the 1980s over concern that thousands of capsules of floating ashes could present a debris hazard to orbiting space vehicles. But Celestis' plan would have the tiny capsules return to Earth again, "harmlessly vaporiz(ing), blazing like a shooting star in final tribute." (AP) ...*Better than slamming into a Space Shuttle's window, perhaps.*

Addicted to Fashion: Two women boarding a flight from Colombia to Miami looked suspicious: both of their dresses sported overly large shoulder pads. Police searched them and found the pads stuffed not with foam, but with 2.5 pounds of heroin. (Reuter) ...*I always wanted to know what a drug "monkey on your back" actually weighed.*

Leftovers Again? "He makes and repairs guitars. He was drunk, sitting in the kitchen with the guitar between his knees, and he slipped," said a Bronx, NY, police detective. Domingo Morales, 67, had told police a prostitute had cut off a portion of his penis when he refused to pay her, but "he did it. It was an accident. He did it himself," detective Sgt. John Kozma said after investigating. The missing part was later found sealed in a food container in Morales' kitchen, but it was too late to be reattached. Morales said he made up the attack story because he was afraid he would be committed to a mental institution if he admitted he cut it off himself. (AP, Reuter, UPI) ...*We'll know if he's insane if he applies as the new spokesman for Tupperware.*

Call Anytime — I'll be There: A Dutch man participating in a trial program wore an electronic tag to prove he stayed in his home on "house arrest" after a conviction for drug dealing found that the test suited him. The good news: he strictly followed the regimen and was home whenever the program required it. The bad news: he spent all his free time dealing drugs to people who visited him at his home. He was arrested after a tip from a customer. (Reuter) ...*There's a lesson here: give good, home-style service, and customers won't turn on you.*

Teacher's Pet Peeve: Dale Davis, an eighth-grade teacher at Largo (Fla.) Middle School, had her students write hate letters to a neighbor she had a dispute with, school officials say. "If you're so worried about her dog having a leash, maybe you should get off your lazy ass and pay for one yourself," one letter said. Davis was reprimanded earlier in the year for "lack of sound professional judgment" in an apparently unrelated case. (AP) ...*She's a genius: she figured out a way to make students want to write!*

Firing on One Cylinder: Robert Overacker, 39, wanted to call attention to the plight of the homeless. He did this by driving a Jet Ski over Niagara Falls. He intended to survive the fall by using a rocket and a parachute, but his plan failed. "His heart was in the right place," a police spokesman said. Friends had earlier tried to stop him from the stunt by removing the spark plugs from the Jet Ski, but Overacker was intent on trying to beat the falls. Only 14 are known to have survived the plunge. "I think the falls is going to win most of the time," one observer noted. (AP) ... *Well, at least he freed up a local apartment.*

Apparently Found

Lost Portrait Of Czar Shown

AP headline

Took His Medicine: James W. Lewis has completed his 12-year federal prison term in El Reno, Okla., for his role in the 1983 "Tylenol murders" case. Cyanide-laced capsules put into medicine bottles on store shelves sent the public into a panic, killed seven unwitting headache sufferers, and dramatically changed the way over-the-counter drugs are packaged. Lewis was a suspect in the deaths, but was convicted only of attempting to extort $1 million from the drug's manufacturer in exchange for a promise "to stop the killing." (AP) *...And just as soon as we can find someone who can figure out how to open the "child proof" cell door, we'll let him out.*

Fat Chance: British researchers say dieting makes people forgetful and "vague", but because of the distraction of the diet, not the reduction in calories. "Constantly thinking about food and worrying about diet means that dieters don't have enough mental processing capacity to deal with tasks properly," said Mike Green of the Institute of Food Research in London. The deficit is about the same as a non-dieting person who consumes two alcoholic drinks. Meanwhile, a researcher from the University of Wisconsin Medical School in Madison says that a diet rich in fat dramatically increases the risk of blindness. (Reuter, AP) *...If I get fat, I won't want to see the numbers on the scale anyway. Or is that fuzzy thinking?*

Cut! A motorist in Dublin saw it all happen: a bank robber shot a guard, then escaped on the back of a motorcycle driven by an accomplice. So he put his car in reverse and was able to thwart their escape by causing them to crash. Unfortunately, the "robbers" were stuntmen, and the getaway was a scene being filmed for television. The motorist "seemed stunned and bewildered," and the film crew reshot the scene so the bad guys would get away, as intended. (Reuter) *...The motorist was "stunned and bewildered"? How about the stuntmen?*

Happy Landings: Three men aboard the Russian space station *Mir* cannot come home as planned on January 13 because the booster rocket for the spacecraft that will bring their replacements up — and them back — hasn't been finished, apparently because of a shortage in construction funding. The new target date: February 21. How do the three cosmonauts feel about the change in plans? "We are going to tell them quite soon, and I am sure they will be pleased about it," a Russian Space Agency spokesman said. (Reuter) *...Yuri, the good news is that you get to avoid the worst part of winter....*

Unclear on the Concept: Charles Mahuka, a Honolulu anger-management counselor who helped people "deal with their abusive impulses", had a bit of a problem with a client who was ordered to attend his class by a family court. The client arrived drunk, witnesses say, and Mahuka allegedly lost his temper over the disruption and beat the man unconscious. Doctors say the victim is brain dead; if declared legally dead, the would-be counselor may be charged with murder. (AP) *...Not all is lost: now they all have a good example to talk about.*

Aim High: The Jockey Club of Southern Africa, which routinely checks the urine of racehorses for illegal substances, indeed found something suspicious in a recent sample: human DNA. Apparently, the horse was unable to provide the sample, so a trainer ordered one of the groomsmen to fill the test container. The official in charge of collecting the sample has been suspended pending an investigation. (Reuter) *...At least they were able to assure him he was clear of any sign of dourine.*

Old Boys' Club: Great Neck, N.Y., attorney Rosalie Osias knew that "mortgage banking is an old-boy network." Yet, she wanted a piece of the action. How to break in? "I needed something sexual to get them to notice," she says, and so her firm tried a new ad campaign. One shows her draped across her desk in a short miniskirt; "Try this nonconforming law firm," the ad urges. "It creates a bad image for lawyers who are already getting a bad rap," complained one male lawyer, critiquing the ad. "Maybe the ads brought in clients, but once they were inside my door, I delivered," Osias countered. Business has gone up by 1000% since the ads started. (AP) ...*This is a bad trend. I don't think I want to see any lawyer's briefs.*

Wait For Me: When William Narr's old girlfriend, Juanita Winston, got out of jail, she went to visit him at the Norristown, Pa., liquor store he managed. She wanted his assurance that they would get back together. When he hesitated, she broke 23 bottles of booze, forced him into a chair, and sat on him until "he finally gave in and told her that he would like to renew their old relationship," court papers say. Winston, who outweighs Narr by 40 pounds, has been charged with assault, reckless endangering and stalking. (AP) ...*So? Is he now visiting her in jail?*

Thanks, Mates: Raymond Rankine escaped from jail in Kununurra, western Australia. Pursuing police spotted him near the Ord River, but he eluded capture by diving into the water. Rankine ignored warnings that a 12-foot crocodile was swimming toward him, so the officers had no choice but to open fire — at the croc. In the ensuing confusion, and with police keeping the crocodile at bay, Rankine completed his escape into the outback. "The last they saw of Rankine, he took off like a hare," a police spokesman said. (Reuter) ...*And they haven't seen hide nor hare since.*

Check Again Later

University Study Says Women, Men Still Different

(Univ. of) Minnesota Daily headline

Go Ahead, Make My Day: Police Chief Eugene Byrd of Isleton, Calif., is under fire from state attorney general Dan Lungren. Once known as the "Asparagus Capital of the World", Isleton is now known as *the* place in Sacramento county to get a permit to carry a concealed handgun, and the fees are the town's third-largest source of revenue. Lungren interprets state law to read that cities can charge a maximum of $3 for a gun permit and has ordered Isleton, which charges $150, to reduce their fee. There is no shortage of applicants: so far this year, 700 permits have been issued, and Byrd's not ready to comply with Lungren's demands. "It's going to take more than some silly threat from the attorney general to scare me," the chief says. "He's going to have to throw me in jail." (L.A. Times) *...Drug dealers and con men operate from jail; no reason Chief Byrd shouldn't be able to too.*

On a Roll: The Philadelphia city employee in charge of stocking Veterans Stadium with toilet paper has been fired. City Controller Jonathan A. Saidel charges the employee used $34,000 in city funds to buy toilet paper, but then apparently sold it, leaving the stadium short before a Philadelphia Eagles football game. "We don't really know how long this was going on," a city spokesman said. "But man, he really wiped that stadium clean." (AP) *...That's it, Saidel: give him his walking papers.*

So That's It: Curious ornithologists wondered why birds indulging in "sexual dalliances" were more likely to produce young than by matings with life-long partners. A study has now shown that the sperm of birds having affairs is speedier, and thus more likely to result in fertilization. The study "ties up a bunch of details on the physiology of... sperm morphology in zebra finches," notes University of Kentucky researcher David Westneat. Male finches were deprived of sex for a week, then presented with freeze-dried females to mate with; the resulting sperm samples were used for the study. (Science News) *...Of course, these results are useless: the researchers didn't take into account that necrophilic finches are likely different from the normal, sexually adjusted bird population.*

Fair Test: Norman Newmarch of Toronto wasn't sure if he had "slept it off" after a bout of drinking the night before. Was he sober enough to drive? To find out, he allegedly drove to an office of the Toronto police department. As he attempted to park in the station's lot, police officers say he hit a parked cruiser. Newmarch was arrested and charged with driving under the influence of alcohol. (AP) *...Sober enough to drive, it seems, but not sober enough to park.*

The Devil Made Them Do It: "What's next, banning Christmas?" demanded one exasperated parent. Indeed, says Los Altos (Calif.) School District Superintendent Marge Gratiot — Christmas was banned a long time ago, along with Hanukkah and Easter. Parents were reacting to the decision to ban the celebration of Halloween in the district's four elementary schools after complaints from Christian fundamentalists, who said such parties violate the Constitution's separation of church — of the devil — and state. "We're restoring values to the schools," insisted Phil Faillace, the school board's president. But faced with hundreds of angry parents, the board voted 4-0 to reverse the ban, and Halloween will return to the Silicon Valley. (AP) *...Why the fuss? No one complained when Christmas, Hanukkah and Easter were banned.*

Economic Theory: Rita Lucas is a long-term planner. When she divorced her husband Robert seven years ago, she had her lawyer insert an unusual requirement into the property settlement: "Wife shall receive 50 percent of any Nobel Prize." Robert, a University of Chicago economist, indeed won the Nobel Prize in economics this month. Will he give her half of the $1 million that comes with it? "A deal is a deal," he said. "It's hard to be unpleasant after winning a prize like that." (AP) *...With foresight like that, she deserves it.*

Can I Quote You? A Florida woman trying to see whether the local Wal-Mart store could beat mail order prices on some items she needed was stopped and told she couldn't write down the store's prices — it was against policy. "I thought they were going to throw me out," Virginia Berger says. Wal-Mart spokesman Keith Morris says the policy is in place to keep competitors from doing price surveys, but Wal-Mart spokeswoman Jane Bockholt says "all customers have the right and are invited to write down prices." Mrs. Berger says Wal-Mart's prices were indeed the lowest she found, "but tough beans" — she doesn't plan to buy the items there, because Wal-Mart has not apologized nor responded to two letters of complaint she wrote to company headquarters. (AP) ...*She'll get two or three letters, just as soon as the PR people duke it out to see who's right.*

Leveled Plains: A city block in Level Plains, Ala., was evacuated while an Army bomb disposal unit was called in to deactivate an "air force missile" that crashed into a back yard shed. Despite speculation that the missile was an errant test warhead from Eglin Air Force Base, 100 miles away, bomb squad technicians determined the "missile" was just an 18-inch toy rocket with air force decals pasted on it. (AP) ...*At least, that's what the brass at Elgin want you to believe.*

No Wonder Kids Are Screwed Up
Women Become More Like Men After Pregnancy —Report
Reuter headline

Eat Your Vegetables! A judge has denied a permit to a "School Dinners" restaurant in downtown Belfast on grounds that it would violate its lease by providing "entertainment". The restaurants (one has been open in London for 14 years) dress their waitresses as English schoolgirls, but with a twist: short skirts, black lace stockings, and whips. The whips are used to "punish" patrons who don't finish their dinners — "entertainment", the judge ruled. "This is not fun, this is filth," says the Rev. Eric Smyth, the lord mayor of Belfast. "Our lord mayor's a fuddy-duddy," answers councilman Sandy Blair, who gave the eatery some publicity by allowing himself to be photographed getting a "spanking" from a waitress. Manager Sally McMullan says she'll try again in another location. (AP) ...*Try Washington D.C., Sally. Our congressmen will eat it up.*

Had to Happen: In the 1980s, the law firm Jacoby and Meyers revolutionized the marketing of legal services through direct consumer TV advertising, and quickly grew to 150 offices in six states. But that success has collapsed: there are only 20 offices now, and — yes — Jacoby has filed suit against Meyers and another partner. Jacoby complains that he was forced out of the firm by a "devastatingly effective squeeze-out technique." Further, his old partners didn't pay his rent, and left him with "severe emotional distress" and "physical and bodily injury, including without limitation headaches and stomach problems." The suit asks for damages of "at least $2 million". (Newsweek) ...*Maybe we can all get a piece of this: their TV commercials caused many headaches and upset stomachs.*

In-Flight Service: A Connecticut investment banker has been charged with assaulting and intimidating a flight attendant and interfering with a flight crew after an episode on a United Airlines flight from Buenos Aires to New York. Flight attendants say they were trying to cut off the allegedly-drunk executive from alcoholic beverage service when he became unruly and shoved a flight attendant. He capped off his antics by dropping his pants and defecating on a food cart, authorities say, then cleaning himself up with the airliner's linen napkins. The banker's attorney says his client, who has been released on $100,000 bail, "vigorously denies the allegations." (AP) ...*Somehow, $100,000 doesn't seem enough.*

Meter Feeder: "Random acts of kindness can be fun," reasoned Cory McDonald, better known as "Mr. Twister" the clown. When walking around the streets of Santa Cruz, Calif., in his clown suit,

Mr. Twister often put money in parking meters so that parked cars wouldn't get overtime tickets. But police found an ordinance on the books prohibiting anyone but the driver of the parked car from putting money in meters, so they ticketed the clown for interfering with their parking enforcement. The clown decided to fight city hall. "The law makes no sense," agreed Mayor Katherine Beiers, and the city council — all wearing clown noses — nullified the ordinance, freeing McDonald from his $13 fine. Mr. Twister is now a local folk hero, and residents are donating quarters to help him feed the meters. (AP) ...*If the cops reasoned it was easier to fight a clown than real criminals, how do they feel now that they've lost?*

In a Lather: Two popular disk jockeys from a San Francisco radio station went to the mayor's house and asked him a question: would he take a shower with them? "People have to know that I have another side too, that I'm not just totally low-key or too serious," Mayor Frank Jordan, 60, says, defending his decision to do it. Jordan, who is up for re-election on November 7, and DJs Mark Thompson and Brian Phelps stood naked in the shower with a microphone, singing Frank Sinatra's "My Way" live on the radio while a photographer snapped photos; one was published in a local paper. "I'm a squeaky clean candidate, and I have nothing to hide," the mayor said. "I think the overwhelming majority of people will see it just for what it is." (Reuter) ...*That depends on where the newspaper cropped the photo.*

Court of Guffaw: Robert Joe Moody, in his trial in Tucson, Ariz., for killing two women, claimed the killings weren't his idea, but rather it was "space aliens" who forced him to take cocaine and kill the women, and that they said he must be convicted and sentenced to death for their experiment to be complete. Then, "after being declared dead, the extra sensory biological entities will bring me back to life to speak through me" to prove he was telling the truth. Moody, a former real estate agent, was declared mentally competent to stand trial and acted as his own attorney. He admits the story "sounds truly bizarre, but the extra sensory biological entities have helped me with certain gifts to understand what's going on." The jury didn't buy it: they convicted him after just two hours of deliberation. (AP) ...*I'm prepared to believe him the minute he comes back to life.*

Truth in Advertising
Marlboro Man Dies Of Cancer
AP headline

Southern Exposure: Brazilian lingerie manufacturer DuLoren has decided not to use a photograph of U.S. First Lady Hillary Clinton in their advertisements. The photographer had been in just the right position to see up Ms Clinton's skirt — her underwear is clearly visible in the resulting photo. "We want [the ad] to say that daring women don't mind letting their their panties be seen," said a spokesman for the agency which created the ad. But DuLoren pulled the ad, noting "The only person that didn't ask that the ad not run was [President] Clinton himself." DuLoren is the same company who hired Hollywood hooker Devine Brown for an ad after she was caught by police in Hugh Grant's car. (Reuter, AP) ...*Well sure Bill wanted to see: it's been a long time.*

The Number's Up: A math professor at the University of California, Irvine, has figured out how to beat lotto. Mark Finkelstein's method involves waiting for the jackpot to pass $18 million, and then betting on the *least*-popular numbers — betting on more popular numbers increases the chance that you'll have to share the jackpot, thus reducing earnings. He estimates his method will, over time, earn a 14% return on the money invested. The catch? It takes 2.3 million years of play to ensure the strategy is profitable. "Actually, I guess you'd be better off with your money in a CD," Finkelstein said. (L.A. Times) ...*2.3 million years? Isn't that about the same time it takes anyway?*

Miracle Child: Severino Antinori, Italy's leading fertility specialist, has confirmed that he has agreed to provide assistance to a Catholic parish priest from Tuscany who is infertile, but wants to have a child. Antinori says the 37-year-old priest, "a handsome young man," told him that "the Old and New Testaments urge all

men to go forth and multiply. They do not specify how." (Reuter)
...But the church has been specific about the hows for centuries.

Seemed Like a Good Idea at the Time: Five years ago, LaVerne
Pavlinac told Oregon police she and her boyfriend had murdered
a woman, even though, she testified at her trial, they really didn't
— she just wanted her boyfriend "off her back". They were both
sentenced to life. Now, the real killer may have been found, and
Pavlinac hopes she'll get her freedom. Is she bitter? No, she says,
but "I'm kind of upset with the way my case wasn't investigated.
They just took my word for it and didn't try to find out anything
else." (AP) *...Funny how they do that.*

European Disunion: Manuel Wackenheim, 28, a Frenchman, has
asked the European Court of Human Rights to overturn a French
court decision that has banned his line of work: he is a dwarf who
has made his living by being "tossed" by patrons in bars and
nightclubs. "Banning him from his work is a restriction of lib-
erty," his lawyer asserts, noting that his 97-pound, 3'10" client
has never been injured. Wackenheim rejects arguments that
dwarf-tossing is a degrading spectacle. "This spectacle is my life;
I want to be allowed to do what I want." (Reuter) *...With a
precedent like this, a lot of professions will have to go.*

Trick or Treat: A police officer in Paulsboro, N.J., wearing a
clown suit over his bulletproof vest, got a lot of treats on Halloween night — a dozen people with outstanding arrest warrants. He
went door to door, asking each time for a fugitive known to live
there. "You don't get a 'He's not home' on Halloween," explained
chief of police Kenneth Ridinger. The idea started two years ago,
when an officer dressed as Batman arrested four people. Police
may take a break next year. "If we do it every year, everybody
will start shutting their doors and the poor kids can't get their
candy," the chief said. (AP) *...Now **there** is a good idea.*

All Systems Go: Stephen Bennett of northern England hopes he
will be the first amateur rocket builder to get a rocket into space,
which by convention starts 75 km above the Earth's surface. He
plans a test November 5; "if it flies and comes back to Earth in
one piece, I've been successful and I will know I can get my next

rocket into space" within a few months, he says. The rocket is fueled by cane sugar. (Reuter) ...*That's nothing: I've seen children on cane sugar reach orbit.*

Tied Up at the Office: San Jose, Calif., suffered a massive case of traffic gridlock Friday when a woman in a bikini was seen whipping a man wearing only a leather G-string at a busy downtown intersection. Officers arrived to find "everything was covered," a police spokesman said. "They weren't breaking any laws, so what could we do?" The couple were participating in a radio station contest to perform the "most outrageous prank". They won. (UPI) ...*Big deal: we see stuff like that in Hollywood every day.*

Lotto Lovin': Stephen Perisie of Riverside, Ohio, and his wife Kim Kay want to put their marriage back together. It may be a long road. Stephen hit the lottery — twice — getting $3 million in 1990 and $100,000 more in 1992. Then Kim Kay hired a man to kill him so she could have all of the lottery winnings. The would-be killer, an undercover police officer, was offered $500 for the killing, and she gave him a $25 down payment. "She tried to be very cheap about this," Stephen notes, but he wants her back: "You don't wash 22 years under the bridge." Kim Kay pled guilty, and is free on bail awaiting sentencing. She faces up to 25 years. (AP) ...*Let go, Stephen: you've just been outbid by the state.*

Better Run, Mum

British Army, Short of Troops, Targets Mothers

Reuter headline

Turn to Page 12: Britain's Methodist Church wants religion to be more "relevant" to children, so their new children's hymnal includes more ...*well*... relevant hymns. "For microchips, for oven chips, computer chips, we thank you Lord ... For floppy disks, for compact discs, computer disks, we thank you Lord," goes one ditty. The hymnal is intended for children under eight. (AP) *...Reverend, Daddy's evil: he won't let me surf the 'net in praise of God.*

Educational TV: "It was disgusting," one 10-year-old student proclaimed. "There were these naked women. Why would they even do that?" His elementary school in Harlem had gathered students to show them the movie "Aladdin", but a porno movie flashed up on the screen instead. Parents were told that the school custodians were likely responsible for the switch, as they had the keys to the film locker and may have swapped the tapes around by mistake. (UPI) *...Oh, sure: blame the janitors rather than admit the teachers can't read the labels.*

What, Again? The world is not going to end. Not on schedule, anyway. Charles Russell, the founder of the Jehovah's Witnesses, first said the world would end in 1914, and only followers would be saved. When that passed by, church officials forecast Armageddon in 1925. Then 1975. Many have been waiting to hear the next prediction, but they will be disappointed: "We do not need to know the exact timing of events," church officials now say. (Reuter) *...Maybe people will believe you if you have a "Going Out of Business" sale.*

Y'all Come Back, Now: Since it had been the mainstay of the local economy, local residents were worried when the West Virginia Penitentiary in Moundsville was closed by the state supreme court, which found the living conditions there "deplorable". What to do? The prison was so notorious that it has been reopened — as a tourist attraction. Visitors can pay $5 to view "Old Sparky", the electric chair used to execute 11 inmates, and the flashpoint of a deadly three-day riot in 1986. "When you walk through there, you have a feeling of, 'Wow, this is really unbelievable how they stayed'," says Phil Remke, spokesman for the Moundsville Economic Development Council. "This is our home and we're not going to let it die on us." (AP) *...A deplorable West Virginia 'home' centered around a deadly chair is a major tourist attraction? And here we figured they wanted to change their state's image, not reinforce it.*

Pull the Chain: Zhengzhou, China, has opened a new public lavatory. But it's no simple outhouse: it has a shower, a marble dressing table, and is decorated with "world famous" paintings — and that's just the ground floor. "On the second floor is a reception room with telephone, fax machine, color television, sound system, air conditioner, sofa, tea table and hot water for making tea," reports the Xinhua news agency. "Though we are losing money currently, we're confident we will make profits in the future because the toilet is located in a busy part of the city," a spokesman for the Public Welfare Service said. The facility cost more than $60,000, and charges an admission fee of two cents. (Reuter) *...One doesn't learn Capitalism overnight.*

Moment of Silence: Students in Alabama's public schools will find a note slipped in with their biology textbooks this year telling them to take evolution with a grain of salt. "No one was present when life first appeared on earth. Therefore, any statement about life's origins should be considered as theory, not fact," the notice reads in part. (AP) *...Galileo couldn't argue with that reasoning either.*

Homeless: Barbie has been kicked out of her Dream House. The Barbie Doll Hall of Fame in Palo Alto, Calif., the world's largest collection (20,000 pieces) of the dolls and accessories, has been evicted from its building, says owner Evelyn Burkhalter. Her lawyer is optimistic that such an important collection will find a new home. "This is really something that has a lot of history to it," attorney Mark Mitchell explained. "It's not like King Tut in a museum." (AP) *...Don't ask me how I can tell, but I think Mark went to public schools.*

Crown Jewels: "The last time any [journalists] thought it was worth coming out here from London was after the time that I tweaked the royal bra strap," Australian Prime Minister Paul Keating reportedly told a reporter from The Guardian, a London newspaper. But Keating denies making the remark. "One expects this sort of behaviour from some British tabloids, but not from a newspaper with the reputation of The Guardian," sniffed a statement issued by his office. Keating was dubbed the "Lizard of Oz" by British newspapers when he put his arm around the queen in 1992. (Reuter) ...*Some guys just can't resist women with a sexy foreign accent.*

Dishonor Student: Peter Koh needed more time to study for a high school calculus test. Just a month after the Oklahoma City terrorist bombing, he figured the best way to stall for time was to rent a Ryder truck, pack it with bags of fertilizer doused with diesel oil, park it in front of his Fort Worth, Texas, high school, and call in a bomb threat. Convicted of making a bomb threat, the former honor student has been sentenced to two years in prison. He never did take his test, and has not been graduated from high school. (AP) ...*You wouldn't think he'd graduate anyway, after four years sitting in a corner.*

Nuclear Recreation: After spending 17 years building a nuclear power plant in Kalkar, the German government bowed to public pressure and decided not to commission it. Now, a Dutch investor is turning it into "Nuclear Water Wonderland" — an amusement park, complete with a roller coaster twisting around the unused cooling towers. The plant cost $5 billion to build, but it was not revealed how much the developer paid for the property. (AP) ...*The snack bar food is the most interesting attraction — it somehow is able to stay warm forever!*

Most of the Night
Census: Unmarried Moms Are Up
AP headline

Sticks and Stones: When psychologist Terrence Webster-Doyle was a kid, he had a problem with bullies. Now, he advises children with the same problem to avoid conflict, but if that doesn't work, "try using humor to defuse the tension or making friends with your tormentor ...or ignoring them," he counsels. If that doesn't work? Try karate, he says. But this advice isn't just for kids: he thinks his methods to defuse conflict can even prevent war. "Conflict is conflict. If you understand it to the basic roots in the playground, you can apply it to adults," he says. (AP) *...Indeed: the only difference between the men and the boys is the destructiveness of their toys.*

On Their Toes: At the recent (New Jersey) State League of Municipalities' annual conference, held this month in Atlantic City, attendees were given a lecture on the "dollars and cents of humor in municipal government". The moderator stressed that humor could help motivate both government officials and the public, and he gave an example of an ice cream company executive who wore a ballerina's costume to pay off a bet he made with employees. "You should try this with mayors who promise to lower taxes," counseled Joey Novick, a councilman from Flemington. "If they don't come through, they have to run around in tights and tutus for a week." (AP) *...But shouldn't they be made to dress in something that makes them appear even sillier than usual?*

Price Fixed: A jury in a U.S. District Court found the defendants of a class-action suit guilty of price fixing in Alabama, but awarded only one dollar to the plaintiffs as a symbolic gesture, not the $6.17 million they sought. But Judge Myron Thompson approved the fees of the 19 lawyers and nine legal assistants who prepared and fought the case: $2,035,658, which the defendant retailers will have to pay. The defendants plan to appeal. (Reuter) *...I'm sure the plaintiffs are considering their own symbolic gesture toward their lawyers.*

A Hole in Her Story: When Sgt. Michael Regan of the Cheltenham Township (Penn.) Police Department made his regular stop for coffee at the Dunkin' Donuts drive-through, he noticed the server got his order wrong. Thinking she maybe didn't actually work there, the suspicious cop pulled out of sight to watch. He called for backup as she escaped through the drive-through service window with money from the register. The 26-year-old woman has been charged with robbery. "If she had given him the right order, maybe she would have gotten away," noted a police spokesman. (AP) *...What really made him suspicious is she asked him to pay.*

Up All Night: A woman arrested for prostitution in Denver was put in a jail cell with 60 men, and had sex with at least two of them, jailers admit. Inmates didn't tip officials off until the next morning. "We've had very effeminate-looking males come into the jail ...including transsexuals and transvestites," a sheriff spokesman said. "Those are things that contributed to the mistake." Officials say the woman was "nonchalant" about the mixup, and no charges are pending, either against the woman or the jailers. (AP) ...*Of course not: there were no crimes involved since she didn't charge for the big-house call.*

Follow Your Nose: Studies show that sperm have the same molecules found in the nose that help detect odors, leading to the theory that sperm "sniff" their way to eggs — and now the hunt is on for the eggs' "perfume". The findings might lead to a new male contraceptive, says Duke University researcher R.J. Lefkowitz. "The idea would be to develop a drug which binds to those receptors," thereby blocking the sperms' ability to pick up the egg scent, she says. "Such a drug could be the ideal contraceptive." (AP) ...*With the interesting Catch-22 side effect being the guy can't smell the woman's perfume, thus making the drug unnecessary — but only to the men using it.*

Black Magic, Black Beauty: Police in Canberra, Australia, are investigating a grisly find: a horse that has been cut in half. "We are investigating a number of possibilities," says a police spokesman. "One that it did involve a satanic ritual" — especially since some satanic-looking symbols were found nearby. However, "Another [possibility] is that it was part of an art show" — since an artistic exhibition had recently been held nearby. (Reuter) ...*The pentagrams were rather arty.*

Happy to See Her: Kevin Hall, 18, apparently wanted to show off for his girlfriend. But when the Bridgeport, Conn., police arrived on the scene, his pants had a large hole in them and he was clutching his groin — from which smoke was rising. He claimed he had been wounded in a drive-by shooting, but his girlfriend provided the real story: he was showing her a gun he had hidden in his pants when it went off, shooting him in ...*um*... a sensitive place. He has been charged with possession of a sawed-off shotgun, reckless endangerment, and the illegal discharge of a firearm. (AP) ...*One of the worst cases of early discharge local doctors have seen in years.*

Out of Uniform
Naked New York City Policeman Quits
AP headline

Dougie Houser, The Miniseries: Michael Kearney is 11 years old, and has a "300-plus" IQ. He has already graduated from college, and is now pursuing an advanced degree at Middle Tennessee State University. A kid this smart must have some plans for the future. "He could be Mozart, Einstein. We have no idea," says his father, Kevin, who educated Michael at home. "Right now he wants to be a game show host." (AP) ...*This may be all the proof we need that TVs in classrooms is a bad idea.*

Close Encounters: Ireland's recent vote on whether to make divorce legal again led to a lot of interesting statistics. "There are 63 percent more UFO sightings in countries with divorce," claimed a poster for the "no" side. "Yes" won with a slight margin. (Reuter) ...*Now we'll never know if they wanted their freedom, or just aspire to see a flying saucer.*

Culture Club: Larry Harris has pled guilty to one count of wire fraud. According to the U.S. Attorney in Columbus, Ohio, Harris falsely claimed he was certified to handle bubonic plague when he mail-ordered a freeze-dried sample of the bacteria from a culture lab. The lab sent the sample, but then turned him in after they got suspicious. Harris, who faces up to six months in jail, wanted the sample as part of his research for a book he was writing about germ warfare, his attorney said. (AP) ...*Makes you wonder what Steven King has in his basement, doesn't it?*

Ugly Waxy Buildup: Madame Tussaud's Wax Museum in London has found the depictions of torture and murder in its Chamber of Horrors aren't graphic enough, so they're updating it to make it more gory. "Children in particular now seem to see far more horrific things on television, so we are totally redoing the chamber," a spokeswoman said. (Reuter) *...A few more years of this, and they won't even react to the real thing. Just like American kids.*

Not in Kansas Anymore: Researchers at the University of Oklahoma have started a study of the way tornados carry debris away from the ground. Historical reports show that paper can be carried more than 200 miles before settling back to earth. But records of such events are sparse, and those they have found "you have to take with a grain of salt," one researcher said. So why bother? They want to create a model "that would be of use to forecasters if a tornado were to hit a hazardous waste site," she said. They have compiled a number of interesting reports so far. A cow was thrown 10 miles in 1878, a pillow went 20 miles in 1913, a jar of pickles traveled 18 miles in 1917, and, in one 1953 storm, trousers went 30 miles and a wedding gown a full 50 miles. (AP) *...Yes, but they had a head start since they were thrown, not just carried off.*

Sniff This: Despite claims that children were not eating their food-scented crayons, the Crayola crayon company has substituted new non-food scents in their markers this year. But an informal test found that children don't agree with the company's descriptions of the odors: the "cedar chest" crayon, for instance, smells instead like "fire" or "DNA" or "dog doo", the "daffodil" is more like "the inside of an airplane", and "leather jacket" more akin to "dead worms", the children said. (Newsweek) *...Better retest: DNA doesn't smell anything like a fire.*

Would You Like Fries With That? "A pound of termites has more nutrients than a pound of beef or pork," says Frank French of Georgia Southern University. He teaches his students that there are more food sources around them than they think. Students are urged to create new recipes using foods such as wild plants, but more points are given if the students use bugs. The catch: students have to eat their creations as part of their assignment. French doesn't shirk his responsibilities: he eats them too. He notes that roasted crickets, for instance, "taste like a fat-laden hors d'oeuvre." However, "the legs aren't very palatable, and the heads are quite objectionable." (AP) *...Mostly, the students learn that the "mystery meat" in the cafeteria may not be so bad after all.*

Hot Spot: Belmont Abbey, near Hereford, England, closed its school for boys last year, leaving the 25 monks with little to do, and the bills piling up to maintain their large buildings. To bring in some cash, they've decided to rent the refectory out for dinner dances and disco nights. But "I don't think any rave-ups will be the order of the day," cautions one of the monks. "We don't want to jeopardize the tranquil nature of our life. Most of our monks will be tucked up in bed" during the parties, he said. (Reuter) *...Father, isn't that just the sort of party you didn't want?*

Chill Out: Two stowaways hoping for free passage from Cape Town, South Africa, to Europe aboard a Norwegian freighter should have read the side of the boat. The "Polar Queen" wasn't enroute to Europe, but to Antarctica. "Not in their wildest dreams had they imagined ending up on the South Pole ice," a ship's officer told a newspaper. "I think it was quite an unusual experience for them." After two weeks, the freighter again sails — back to Cape Town. (AP) *... "There is nothing — absolutely nothing — half so much worth doing as simply messing about in boats."* —*Ken Grahame*

Inside Job

Prison Loses Master Key for Cells

Reuter headline

Could Have Had a V-8: James P. Maynard, 22, was driving through Charleston, W. Va., with two friends. They were playing a game while he drove. Russian Roulette. "He pointed the gun at one guy, and it clicked. He pointed it at his own head and it clicked," says a police spokesman. "The third time he pulled it, it went off." The car, with its driver shot in the head, went out of control and crashed into a wall. Maynard is in critical condition and the two passengers were injured. (AP) ...*Maybe now kids will understand just how important it is to wear seatbelts.*

May I Use Your Pen? The Movement for Restoration of Peace and Order, a crime-watch organization of ethnic Chinese in Manila, says that kidnappers in the Philippines have become so brazen that they now accept checks for ransom. Many of the 155 people kidnaped for ransom in the Philippines this year were Chinese, they say, and paid off their kidnappers with checks ranging from $11,500 to more than $38,000. "I doubt if [the victims] gave stop-payment instructions because the kidnappers would certainly have gotten back to them," says an MRPO spokesman who wouldn't give his name. (Reuter) ...*What do you mean I need two forms of identification?!*

It's the Thought that Counts: Giving the gifts of "The 12 Days of Christmas" is cheaper this year, according to a study by the PNC Bank of Pittsburgh. Thanks in part to "a 50 percent drop in the cost of seven swans-a-swimming," notes the bank's director of economic and equity research, and despite an increase in the cost of Lords-a-Leaping, giving all the gifts implied by the song now costs just $51,764.94, down 29.42 percent from last year. (They note, though, that local prices may vary and, because "it doesn't take into account if your true love lived far away," shipping and handling are not included.) The bank compiles the cost annually in part, says PNC economist Rebekah Fickling, "to prove that occasionally us economists do have a sense of humor." (AP) ...*So much for the idea that economists are just numbers people that don't have enough personality to be accountants.*

Obscene and Not Heard: America Online has reversed part of its new policy to ban the "use of obscene or vulgar language" in messages posted by customers of the online service after breast cancer victims complained they couldn't discuss their disease online because "breast" was on the company's "vulgar word" list. "Give us a break! Must we have 'hooter cancer survivors'?"

demanded one woman before AOL started allowing "breast" to be used again. "I don't consider 'breast' to be a dirty word," says a spokeswoman for the American Cancer Society. "If you have people who see it as dirty, for whatever reason, rather than as an everyday term, then this is going to continue to happen," she said. (AP) ...*Funny: I never thought it was the words that were dirty.*

Safe Sex: London International Group Plc, one of the world's largest manufacturers of condoms, has taken to the Internet. Their "Ins and Outs of Sex: everything you ever needed to know about condoms and safer sex" web site offers "an interesting, fun and interactive way to learn about condoms, romance and safer sex, while educating [visitors] about the benefits of Durex condoms," a spokesman said. (Reuter) ...*Who would bother with online sex? You can't type when you only have one free hand.*

Offerings They Can't Refuse: Two of Italy's oldest and largest institutions — the Roman Catholic Church and the Mafia — have begun to clash. The Pope has exhorted the Mafia to stop murdering people, but some priests think that just isn't enough. "We've condemned the Mafia. OK. What do we do now?" asks the Rev. Cosimo Scordato. Rev. Antonio Dell'Olio adds that the church must do more, such as have prison chaplains work to convert imprisoned Mafiosi, and stop reserving front-row church service seats for gangsters. (AP) ...*That's not special treatment — that's keeping an eye on troublemakers.*

Talk of the Town: "I'm just not accustomed to things like this happening," said one family member. "I watch it on 'Geraldo'." She was referring to William Douglas Hinson, 71, and his granddaughter, Teresa Jean Hutcheson, 30. During a 20-year relationship, Hinson fathered two of his own great-grandchildren with Hutcheson. But that's not what brought the relationship into the public eye in Myrtle, Miss., population 350. Rather, it was the conspiracy between the two to kill the woman's husband, Dean, for his life insurance money. "In my 20 years on the bench, I thought I'd seen everything," noted U.S. District Judge Neal Biggers, sentencing both to the maximum prison terms — five years — after they pled guilty to the plot. "If I could give you 20 years,

I would." Dean has filed for divorce. (AP) ...*Not good enough for Geraldo. If the grandfather was once a woman, and the husband a cross-dressing stripper who wanted the marriage to continue, then maybe. Just maybe.*

Terrible Twos: Two women attending a class at the Brunswick County (Virginia) Public Schools Learning Center have been expelled from the class for fighting. After starting to argue over a "mutual male acquaintance", one ran out to her car and returned with a steak knife and has been charged with assault and possession of a weapon on school property. The other was charged with assault; both were released after posting bond. The class the women were taking? "How to be better parents." (AP) ...*They apparently missed the prerequisite requirements.*

Stoplifter: Security guards at a department store in Manila noticed a 20-year-old man walking out the front door without any shopping bags. What caught their eye was an "unnatural swell" in the man's crotch. A search revealed five bras stuffed into the front of his pants. He has been charged with theft. (Reuter) ...*Yeah, 10 breasts in a man's pants sounds like reasonable "probable cause" for a search.*

Yes! I Can See It!
Scientists Find 'Mind's Eye'
Reuter headline

Appointed Rounds: Two mail carriers in Bergenfield, N.J., are having a contest to see which can go the longest delivering mail wearing their summer uniform — shorts. The winter competition is far from over: it has lasted 14 months so far. "We just keep going and going," says Ron Filera, 26. "It's been a little chilly, but the key is to keep moving." The postmaster isn't too concerned. "If it gets really, really cold, we'll tell them to put their pants on," he notes. The bet's stakes have doubled this year, to two cases of beer. (AP) ...*Anything that keeps the mail moving briskly is OK.*

Give Them What They Want: Sylvia Branzei, a California school teacher, got her inspiration while clipping her toenails. "I said, 'Ooh, what's this icky stuff under my toenails?'," she remembers. Then, "it hit me that there's a lot of gross things about our body that we want to know about." Just out is her new book, "Grossology", which explains most everything that oozes, runs, or otherwise comes out of a person's body. The book even comes with a magnifying glass so children "can analyze their own bodily discharges". The book is selling well. "I write a book about boogers and farts and I'm sitting on a gold mine," Branzei says. "I never thought this was what America wanted." (AP) ...*She hasn't been to very many movies lately, then.*

Not Enough Evidence: Brice Hubbard, on trial in Lexington, Ky., on a child abuse charge, heard testimony in court from the 9-year-old victim that he had spots on his genitals. So, in his defense, Hubbard stood before the jury and dropped his pants so that they could see that he did not. "The jury took it very serious," Judge James Keller noted. But at the end of the trial, the jury couldn't reach a verdict, so Keller declared the jury hung. (AP) ...*Apparently, the defendant wasn't.*

Take Off Your White Coat: Karen Hopkin admits she "had the idea for the calendar so that I myself could meet guys." But it's not just any beefcake calendar: Hopkin is the producer of National Public Radio's "Science Friday" show, so her calendar is "Studmuffins of Science". "If you have a Y chromosome and a Ph.D., you could be Dr. December!", she advertised. "For the sake of science, you have to do it," said Dr. September's wife, when he told her he had won one of the 12 spots in the calendar. Dr. September — Brown University researcher Robert Valentini — thinks the idea "is to make science and medicine more approachable... to make scientists look like real people instead of nerds in the lab who have white coats and play with mice." (AP) ...*At least, that's what he told his wife.*

Can't Touch This: Britain's Literary Review awarded its annual "Bad Sex Prize" this year to Philip Kerr's "Gridiron". The award recognizes literary descriptions of lovemaking that are "redundant, perfunctory, unconvincing, embarrassed and embarrassing, as well as unacceptably crude," a spokesman said. Kerr's "His tremulous thumbs gathered the elastic waist of her panties and plucked them down over the twin golden domes of her behind and back up over the suspended sentences and Sobranie filter-tips of her stocking-tops as, obligingly, she brought her knees up to her chest" apparently met the criteria. Kerr defended his writing. "I think it's rather poetic in a way," he said, adding "Any sex is good sex." (Reuter) ...*At least, that's what he tells his wife.*

Fighting Words: Johnny Mathis, 20, noticed that a police car parked in front of a restaurant in Portland, Maine, had a dog in the back. Police said he started to tease the dog, who then started barking. So Mathis barked back. Officers were not amused: they arrested him on a charge of taunting a police dog, a misdemeanor. "I had finished barking. I had stopped barking, and the police still arrested me," Mathis complains. (AP) ...*Don't whine: it shows poor training.*

Aw, Shoot: Game Warden Joseph Dedrick could hardly wait. On his day off, he went quail hunting, and bagged a bird. But, a friend noted, pointing to a game department brochure, quail season doesn't start for another week. "I called my lieutenant the next morning and told him, 'We're going to have to get a warrant on me'," Dedrick says. He charged himself with hunting out of season, and was fined $25 plus court costs. (AP) ...*Now there's a cop who won't buy any excuses.*

For the Birds: "My entire life has changed from joy and happiness to sadness and depression," says Ruby Campagna of Roanoke, Va. She enjoyed watching baby birds in a nest outside her apartment window. But the apartment manager, Judy Woody, made a practice of removing bird nests from the property. Campagna filed suit when Woody removed the nest by her window. Woody, "a malevolent scowl on her face," knocked the nest down then stepped on it "in order to mutilate and mangle their tiny bodies," her suit said. Woody says she didn't know there were baby birds in the nest when she knocked it down, but a Roanoke Circuit Court jury awarded Campagna $135,000 for her "emotional distress and medical bills". (AP) ...*Is that compensation for distress, or an award for creative writing?*

Isn't That the Usual Way?
Family Jewels Lost in Mistake
AP headline

Let Me Show You: The Grand Blanc (Mich.) Township Fire Department wanted to show just how dangerous Christmas tree fires can be, so they set up a tree in an abandoned house and set it afire for camera crews from two local TV stations. The fire spread out of control, and the cameramen had to run for their lives. Unfortunately, they got entangled in their camera equipment and fell; both were burned, one seriously. Two firefighters were also injured. (AP) ...*Remember, they're experts: don't try this at home.*

Let Me Show You II: Scott Plumley was upset about drug dealing in his neighborhood in Pensacola, Fla., but police said they needed proof of the activity before they could do anything. So Plumley summoned officers to his house to show them a $4 bag of marijuana he bought near his home. "After I bought it, I thought 'There it is. Boom! Now get him off the street'," Plumley said. Police took action all right: they arrested Plumley for possession of marijuana. (AP) ...*And, police note, complaints about drug dealing on that street have since dropped dramatically.*

Smooooth! "If you irradiate good wine or whisky, they taste terrible. But if you expose bad wine and cheap whisky to gamma rays, they taste much better," says Hiroshi Watanabe, of the Japan Atomic Power Company's research lab in Takasaki. Just 2,000 joules of gamma rays — about 250 times the lethal dose for humans — "promotes the blending process, and that takes away any aftertaste," Watanabe says. (Reuter) ...*And, glow-in-the-dark drunks wouldn't be run over as often at night.*

His Humble Opinion: A reporter following up on a story about the Equal Employment Opportunity Commission's order that the "Hooters" restaurant chain must also hire men to wait tables went to a Hooters in Charlotte, N.C., to interview patrons. One apparent regular, James Posey, wasn't shy about expressing his opinion. "The whole concept of Hooters would be undermined if they had to hire male waiters. The girls are basically what Hooters is about," he said. But when it was revealed later that Posey is better known as the Rev. James Posey of Woodlawn Baptist Church, he resigned his pulpit, noting he is "frustrated over the lack of growth at Woodlawn". (AP) ...*Sounds like the flock was just following its leader, rev.*

Plan B: John Albert Taylor, sentenced to death in Utah for the rape and murder of an 11-year-old girl, surprised authorities when he chose a firing squad as his method of execution, rather than lethal injection. Especially since they have no procedures set for it, nor a place to do it. "You need to find a shooting area and give the firing squad a chance to practice in those conditions," says a former warden who set up the state's last firing squad, in 1977. "I think it is fair to say we're going to be involved in a fair amount of innovation," a prison spokesman said, noting that there isn't anyone assigned to a firing squad, and a call for volunteers will have to be issued. Critics are distressed at the timing — Utah is trying to attract the 2002 Winter Olympics to the state. (AP) ...*A smart public relations agency would simply bill this as biathlon practice.*

Where's the Fire? Stephen Coleman, 25, really didn't want a speeding ticket. Police in Portsmouth, R.I., pulled him over for going 56 mph in a 25 zone, but, when the officer started writing a ticket, police say Coleman jumped in his car and sped off. When finally cornered, Coleman allegedly jumped out of his car, punched out two patrolmen, and, when they tried to subdue him with pepper spray, dove into the nearby Sakonnet River and refused to come out. Police were not about to go in after him: this time of year, the water is icy. Two fire rescue divers in cold suits finally dragged him out, and Coleman is in intensive care suffering from hypothermia. Police are apparently not concerned with Coleman's speeding, but they are planning to charge him with eluding, assaulting and obstructing police officers, reckless driving, and resisting arrest. (AP) ...*If they let him get away with* *speeding, there's no reason for him not to do it again.*

Something About John: First, Post Office officials say, John Pitney, 50, came to work at the downtown Denver mail processing facility wearing a dress. Postal authorities escorted him off the premises and ordered him not to return. But return he did, wearing not only the dress, but also a gorilla mask and "a strap-on sexual device". When he returned a second time, police were called in. They found several guns in his car, and took him in for psychiatric evaluation. (AP) *...It's about time postal officials have started to notice the subtle little warning signs when their people crack up.*

Pull in Case of Emergency: "Never make a mess of the legendary Santa laugh. Too much 'Yo' and not enough 'Ho' is a common mistake," lectures Tom Valent, known as one of the best Santa trainers in the world. He was flown from the U.S. to England to teach Santas there how to act. "British children are often left cold by characters who look more like Santa Flaws than Santa Claus," said a spokesman for the group which hired him. "Santa is not a disciplinarian. If a child pulls your beard then laugh," he said. (Reuter) *... 'Yo'? That's the pirate school, down the hall.*

I Hear You: Stevon Sutton and Emmett Wallace got in a fight in a bar in Fort Wayne, Ind., police say, and Sutton bit off Wallace's ear — and never spit it out. When police arrived, they say he would not give the ear back, though he did stick it out of his mouth several times, and then sucked it back in. When officers tried to retrieve it, Sutton swallowed it. "This is a first, definitely a first," a police spokesman said. Sutton was arrested, but after a search for laws regarding cannibalism — and finding none — Sutton was charged with battery and criminal recklessness. (AP) *...Time for a new law: contemptible public grossness.*

Pillars of Science

Geologists Find Sodom; Explain Lot's Salty Wife

Reuter headline

What's That Under the Tree? Roger Sallberg, who owns a forest in southern Sweden, has tired of people poaching trees from his land each Christmas. He has finally figured out how to get even: he pours raw sewage on the branches. When the trees are taken inside the thieves' houses and their icy cargo thaws, the odorous payload drips on the rug. (Reuter) ...*A lot of innocent dogs will be in trouble on Christmas morning.*

Christmas Gratings: President Clinton sent a Christmas greeting card to the Alabama Governor's mansion. The card was neatly addressed to Alabama's Governor Jim Folsom, a Democrat. "Either they haven't gotten word of the election last November, or perhaps they're in denial," notes a spokesman for the governor, Fob James, a Republican who defeated Folsom for the post more than a year ago. "It looks like we're working off a bad list here," admitted a spokesman for the president. (AP) ...*He's an amateur — experts check their lists twice.*

Spirits of Christmas: Eighteen people on a flight from London to Los Angeles were detained upon their arrival after allegedly going on a drunken rampage on the airplane. When flight attendants tried to cut them off from the booze, they allegedly sent children to the galley to raid the liquor cabinet. Three of the passengers had to be subdued by members of the U.S. Olympic Wrestling Team, who happened to be traveling on the flight. "At one point we had to handcuff them. It got out of control," one team member noted. Seventeen of the passengers were sent back to England; the other has been detained on federal charges. (Reuter) ...*He kept saying he needed a red nose to help guide the plane that night.*

This One Looks Good: Two robbers decided to hit Z's Sports Tap, a bar in downtown Chicago. "Much to the chagrin of the two stickup people, there was a retirement party going on," a police spokesman says — a Chicago Police retirement party. At least 100 off-duty officers were there, making the bar so crowded that the robbers lured the bartender outside — away from the till — to rob him. "That's what makes this job so interesting," one officer said. "Dumb people." (AP) ...*Not so dumb: they told him* *to bring his checkbook.*

They're Dead, Jim: English researchers studying fans of "Star Trek" have found that 10 percent or more are obsessive about the TV series, even showing withdrawal symptoms "when insufficient Star Trek activities are encountered." Some, the sociologists from the University of Northumbria say, even dream about the show's characters and argue plot points. (Reuter) ...*Next week, we'll find out that there are actually sports fans who dress up in uniforms of their favorite teams, and even memorize detailed statistics about the players.*

High Court: "Anyone who uses drugs is an idiot, but I do not feel it is an illegal matter," Cleveland Judge Michael Gallagher once told a reporter. Gallagher has now pleaded guilty to charges of distributing cocaine after trying to convince an undercover federal drug agent to sample his wares at his home. Gallagher now faces up to 20 years in prison, $1 million in fines, and the "possible" loss of his license to practice law. (AP) ...*Apparently he was right when he said druggies were idiots.*

Nutty Professor: A doctor from Liverpool University says that a popular children's animal book character was suffering from a neurological disorder. Squirrel Nutkin, hero of a book by Beatrix Potter, "does seem pathologically challenged," said Dr. Gareth Williams. "While the other squirrels foraged for food and were being deferential to the owl, Nutkin indulged in solitary activities such as repetitive toying with pine needles and playing marbles or ninepins," he wrote in the British Medical Journal. His conclusion: Tourette's syndrome. "I started looking into this after I read the story to my six-year-old son and he kept asking whether Squirrel Nutkin was all right," he said. (Reuter) ...*What kind of disorder is it when a physician diagnoses problems in fictional characters?*

Just Call Me Jim-Bobby: Due to a loophole in state law, three convicted felons not only were allowed to run for but won posts as county sheriffs in Mississippi. "This really makes us look kind of dumb. I can only believe that many voters did not know the situation," lamented Public Safety Commissioner Jim Ingram.

State Attorney General Mike Moore notes that state law prohibits ex-felons from carrying firearms, and that the new lawmen will be arrested if they try to carry guns once they take office. How will they face down criminals if they can't carry guns? "That's something I don't want to get into now," one of the new sheriffs said. (AP) ...*Maybe they have time for some training sessions in England.*

Flipped Their Lids

Headless Humans Could be a Design Improvement: Doctor

Australian AP headline

Working for Supper: Richard Gardner, 23, and his wife were at his mother-in-law's house in South Carolina for Christmas dinner when their hostess asked him to fix some loose molding. Unable to fix it by hand, he grabbed a .25-caliber pistol to use as a hammer. The gun went off, shooting his wife and injuring his hand. Both have been released from a local hospital. (AP) ...*Brilliant: they'll never dare to ask him to help around the house again!*

Drop in Anytime: Psychiatrist Dennis Tison was in a small boat near San Francisco's Bay Bridge with his cell phone, a camera, and a life jacket when a man hit the water nearby. "I asked him if he jumped from the bridge, and he said, 'Yes, get me out of here!'," Tison said later. The shrink tossed the man his life jacket, called for help on his phone, and snapped a few photos. Did he also use his skills to provide counseling to the man? Tison didn't say. (AP) ...*Doctor-patient confidentiality is sacred, you know.*

Adventures at Sea II: The Italian air force rescued five fishermen stranded in a life raft in the Bay of Naples. But when police heard one of them whisper "the guards haven't noticed anything" in a phone call to his wife from a Naples hospital, they investigated. He turned out to be Francesco Pizzimenti, a fugitive wanted on charges of drug smuggling. He was arrested and transferred to jail. The other four men were released despite their own criminal records. (Reuter) ...*Good fishermen know to throw a few back for later trips.*

True Spirit of Christmas: The K Foundation, a London charity, wanted to bring a special warmth to the homeless for Christmas. Noting that most liquor outlets close for the holiday, they passed out 6,237 cans of beer. "If you are down and out, would you rather have a bowl of soup or a can of Tennent's?" asked K's founder, Jimmy Cauty. (AP) ...*One really needs something from* **each** *of the four food groups: alcohol, sugar, salt and fat.*

True Spirit of Christmas II: A 13-year-old Texas boy is in custody after shooting a man driving on the freeway. The boy was trying to shoot out the tires of a passing truck with a rifle so that it would tip over and spill its load — the boy imagined the truck contained Nintendo games, and he wanted one for Christmas, his brother said. The truck driver didn't notice the shots, but the driver of a nearby pickup was hit in the head by one bullet and is in critical condition. The boy has been charged with deadly conduct. (AP) ...*If he wanted a Nintendo that bad, maybe he should have sold his rifle.*

Oliver's Twist: Michael Ross, 13, told authorities he was abandoned by his parents at a Utah bus stop just before Christmas. But when he fled a foster home rather than submit to a medical examination, they found the problem: "Michael" was actually Birdie Jo Hoaks, a 25-year-old woman who was trying to find a warm place to stay during the holidays. And, investigators allege, she had previously used the scam in as many as 18 other states. "If a proper medical exam had been conducted early on, we certainly would not have gotten so far and deep into this," explained an attorney assigned to represent the interests of the "boy". Hoaks has been charged with forgery and making false statements, and faces five years in prison. (AP) ...*Just what she wanted: a warm place to stay for awhile.*

Petrol Power: Los Angeles' Catholic Cardinal Roger M. Mahony anointed a gas station in Oakhurst, Calif., even stopping to bless a cigarette advertisement depicting the Marlboro Man. "Our God created the world and filled it with marvelous signs of his power," the Cardinal said. Mahony said it was his idea to do the blessing at the station, which is owned by friends. (AP) ...*Well, if God created everything, that would include lung cancer.*

Taxpayers Cry over Sour Milk: Researchers at Purdue University, funded by a half-million-dollar U.S. Department of Agriculture grant to study the mood of livestock, report that dairy cows do not like music by the rock group Kiss, but do like Mozart. They say such research on the cows, as well as chickens and pigs, is important since, for example, happy cows produce more milk than grumpy cows. (AP) ...*Wouldn't a truer test of its worth be to see if farmers will support it with their own money?*

Ate Eight: Caribou has become a popular main course in restaurants over the last few years. Not familiar with it? It's better known as reindeer. "During the Christmas holidays I don't think it's a good idea to call it reindeer," says Loretto Sanguinegti, a chef at a Jackson Hole, Wyo., restaurant where it has become popular. "I think ['caribou'] rolls off the tongue a little bit better," agrees a Chicago specialty meat distributor. "People think of reindeer, they think of Santa Claus." Most of the reind— ...*er...* caribou comes from Alaska. (AP) ...*Sometimes it's sad to see the results of post-season layoffs at the North Pole.*

But Let's Not Jump to Conclusions
Maybe Error Led to Air Crash
AP headline

Give Us 5–10, We'll Take Off the Weight: Wayne Garner, Georgia's new commissioner for prisons, has some changes he'd like to make. First, the prisoners aren't in good enough shape, and will be forced to exercise. There's "30 to 35 percent that ain't fit to kill," he says. He plans to make them dig ditches, then fill them back in. "When they get out, they're not going to want to come back," he said. (AP) ...*You would think the local residents would* *prefer their violent inmates to be fat and slow.*

Win Some, Lose Some: Andre-Francois Raffray, a lawyer from Arles, France, thought he had made the deal of a lifetime. In 1965, he signed a contract with Jeanne Calment, then 90 years old, giving her $500 a month for life on condition that she leave him her house when she died. On Christmas, Raffray died at 77, shortly after Calment became the world's oldest known living person — she'll be 121 in February. "We all make bad deals in life," Raffray said on Calment's 120th birthday. He paid her over $180,000 in the deal; the house is worth about $60,000. (Reuter) *...Getting to beat a lawyer would give anyone a strong reason to live.*

Crass Action Suit: Patricia McColm of San Francisco filed so many lawsuits against her neighbors that real estate agents were required to warn people moving into the area about her. Now, she has been declared a "vexatious litigant" by a judge. Under the judge's order, she cannot file any more lawsuits without permission, and must post a bond covering the defendant's legal fees should she lose the case. "We had a crack dealer with a pit bull and weapons," one neighbor said. "It was easier and less anxiety-producing getting rid of him." McColm filed dozens of suits over neighbor children playing in their yards (too noisy), a door that hit her in the foot, and for miscellaneous alleged injuries sustained in nine auto accidents. She even went to law school to help her legal campaign, but when she twice failed the bar exam, she sued the State Bar for emotional distress. "You are the most vexatious vexatious litigant I have ever dealt with," said the judge who applied the order. (S.F. Chronicle) *...I'll sue you for that! That is, if you'll kindly give me permission to.*

Designated Driver: Donald Stevens had allegedly been drinking, and knew it wasn't a good idea to drive. So he had his son, 12, drive him home. When police in Riverside County, Calif., spotted the pair and tried to pull them over, Stevens told the boy "not to stop, just slow down and drive home." Police followed the car all the way to Stevens' home — at 15 mph — and arrested him on charges of public intoxication, allowing an unlicenced juvenile to drive, and possession of a controlled substance. (AP) ...*He was lucky: they could have charged him with back seat driving under the influence.*

Holiday Blowout Sale: Charlotte's, a London soft goods and furniture store, had a holiday sale. But owner Martin Barnett found sales beat all expectations: a sheikh from Qatar bought everything in the store — including the floor, the cash register, and the wallpaper from the wall. "Apparently, his third wife had been in during the summer and he said she liked the concept," Barnett said. The sheikh paid 350,000 pounds — about US$544,000. (Reuter) ...*What do you mean that doesn't include the sales girls?*

Break a Leg: Opera singer Richard Versalle, 63, was on stage at the Metropolitan in New York to sing the opening of "The Makropulos Case". Versalle fell dead to the stage after he sang the line "You can only live so long." The Met dropped the curtain and canceled the performance. (AP) ...*More proof that Method Acting should be outlawed.*

Doggie Bag: Karen McInulty, 29, had a chicken curry dinner in an Indian restaurant near Edinburgh, and ended up with a bad case of salmonella poisoning. She was in a hospital for a week, and couldn't return to work for two months. A court ordered the restaurant to pay her 3,700 pounds (US$5,700) in compensation, but the restaurant owner appealed: she was overweight, he said, and thus the 21-pound weight loss resulting from her illness was good for her. An appeals court rejected the argument. (Reuter) ...*He sounds like a fathead; maybe he'd like to try that diet himself.*

Mother Never Purred: Researchers at New York's Cornell University are developing personality tests for cats. "Some people want an animal that will sit and watch them work. Other people want a cat that will catch mice," explained Soraya Juarbe-Diaz in the journal New Scientist. The test measures kittens' reactions to being petted, to silhouettes of dogs and other cats, and to recordings of barking and meowing. (Reuter) ...*I just want a cat that doesn't think he's smarter than me.*

Flushing Bride
Taiwan Lovers Plan
Bathroom Nuptials
Reuter headline

Help Wanted: Walter Thiele, 75, of Tegernsee, Germany, wants the best for his wife, Renate, who is 28 years old. "She is young, beautiful and full of lust for life," he says, and he doesn't want her to be lonely when he dies. So he's searching for a man to take care of her when he goes — and the millions of dollars he made on his invention, a small battery-operated machine in a bag which laughs at the push of a button. Hundreds of men have applied for the task. (Reuter) ...*Gee, Walt, with millions of dollars and a few battery-operated machines, you would think she could take care of herself.*

Now Hear This: When the passenger subway between terminals at Denver's new airport stalled last week, airport officials suddenly realized they had no way to talk to the stranded passengers to tell them what to do. Airport managers told the City Council that the lack of a public address speaker system was a "weak spot" in the design. The city bought bullhorns to use for emergencies until a PA system can be installed. Meanwhile, airport officials are embarrassed that they accidentally impounded and towed away the car of their local member of the House of Representatives, Pat Schroeder. Her car had been in the 30-day lot for less than 20 days. (AP, 2) ...*She likely won't need a bullhorn to make officials hear what she has to say about that.*

Tourist Distraction: The "World's Largest Peanut", a three-foot, 50-pound metal monument to the roasted pea on "prominent" display in front of city hall in Durant, Okla., was stolen last September. But police weren't called until last week. "We didn't even know it was missing until some tourists told us about it," admits City Clerk Tommy Bradburn. Publicity led to a tip to police, who recovered the treasure and questioned three suspects.

(AP) *...It's the first time they needed a sledge hammer to crack a case.*

I Want to Tell You: The producer of a video in which O.J. Simpson professes his innocence in the stabbing murder of his ex-wife and a friend is threatening to sue people who try to thwart its sale. At least one Los Angeles radio station suggested that listeners call the distributor's toll-free number and ask questions so others couldn't get through to order the $30 tape; the suggestion has also spread on the Internet. Producer Tony Hoffman says he has printed out all Internet messages calling for such action, and has directed the company providing his toll-free telephone service to record the numbers of repeat callers so that they can be sued. "Our attorneys are right now preparing litigation," Hoffman says. (AP) *...Apparently Tony would rather be known as a laughingstock than an O.J. apologist.*

Call Us if You Need a Ride: California authorities say Maliu Mafua, 27, walked away from a minimum security jail. He stopped at a pay phone to call a friend but didn't know the number, so he called for directory assistance — 411. But instead, he accidentally dialed the emergency number — 911. He quickly hung up, but police responded anyway and found him still in the phone booth, still wearing a shirt emblazoned "Property of San Mateo County Honor Camp". Housed now in the more-secure county jail, Mafua pleaded not guilty to felony escape charges. (AP) *...If you can't get him on that, try theft of jail clothing.*

Buster Brown: Shoe maker Adidas America has rejected a call from President Clinton's anti-drug "czar" Les Brown to change the name of their popular new shoe, "Hemp". The shoes are called that because they're made from the reedy plant, not to glorify marijuana use. "Products made from hemp, including our shoes, have no drug qualities. I don't believe you will encounter anyone smoking our shoes anytime soon," replied Adidas president Steve Wynne. (AP) *...It's not necessary to smoke them. The vapors alone can cause altered states of consciousness.*

M.C. Gavel: Police raiding a hideout of two suspected burglars found $30,000 worth of stolen merchandise, and a surprise: a rap video the pair allegedly made with a stolen video camera. The two, who rap about using drugs and how "crime pays in many ways," face charges stemming from a three-week smash-and-grab spree in Buffalo, N.Y. One suspect sang to the camera, "I'm learning my acting skills. I want you to sit back and enjoy the show. Eat some popcorn and drink some beverages." (AP) ... *That is a crime / the guy don't rhyme / make him do a lot of time.*

I'll be in the Waterworld Suite: The Australian National Parks and Wildlife Service wasn't quite sure what to do with six small whales which beached themselves near Crescent Head, north of Sydney. They pulled them out to sea, but they came back and beached themselves again. So officials asked a nearby hotel if they could use their saltwater pool. "The pool isn't being used at the moment because of the weather so they are quite welcome to stay," the hotel manager said. Hotel guests are swimming with the mammals and helping them back to health. (Reuter) ... *Checking out? Let's see: six guests for six nights, plus room service....*

See You in the Alley at Noon: Conservative newspaper columnist William Safire says he is grateful to President Clinton for providing him with "historic notoriety". When Safire said in his column Monday that the president's wife is a "liar," Clinton threatened a "forceful response to the bridge of Mr. Safire's nose." Safire said the threat gave him more circulation — with the blizzard blanketing the east, "hardly anybody in Washington received that issue of the paper." (AP) ... *The president immediately departed for Oxford so he wouldn't have to fight.*

Can You Identify Yourself? Britain's record 42 million-pound (US$65 million) lottery jackpot was split three ways last week. One winner is a Chinese man who flew into London to claim his part of the winnings. Simon Choy Tat Sai collected his 14 million-pound check and returned to China the next day. But British newspapers suspect the man's name is a pseudonym: they say it translates to "vegetable getting rich". Lottery officials will only say that "our winners have requested no publicity." (Reuter) ... *He may be a vegetable, but he's not stupid.*

Multimedia: Singapore's Law Society has produced a CD-ROM program on youth crime which features a graphic demonstration of caning. "We heard the sound of the cane followed by the scream," said one student who saw the disk. "It was so scary that we were speechless." A parting shot shows the mark the cane made on the prisoner's naked buttocks. "The CD-ROM is not preachy. It doesn't tell you not to commit crimes, it shows you the consequences," one director of the Law Society said. The computer disk has already been distributed to Singapore schools, and the Law Society is now trying to sell the disk through bookstores for S$35 (US$18). (UPI) ...*That's nothing: the next disk in the series is the Islamic Law Society's CD-ROM on crime and punishment.*

Sale Ends Tuesday
NATO Discounts Rocket Firing
AP headline

Sea Hunt: How do you reconcile catch-and-release rules with fishermen who want to display their catches on their den walls? Enter the plastic fish. Taxidermists are now offering acrylic replicas of fish, rather than preserving the real thing. "No one would ever know it wasn't real if I didn't tell them," one fisherman claims, showing off his trophy. But credibility suffers with repetition. "We have a mold of a world-record largemouth bass that's more than 20 pounds. That's a popular one, but it's not likely that that many people caught it," says one Ohio taxidermist who has sold copies many times. "When they're paying the bill," another said, "if they want a 12-pound fish instead of a 5-pound fish, it doesn't matter to me." (AP) ...*Not impressive: trophy on wall. Impressive: great fish dinner.*

Crow Magnons: Massey University (New Zealand) researcher Gavin Hunt says that crows living in New Caledonia's rain forests use tools at about the same level as Stone Age humans. "I observed an adult with both food and a tool in its bill land next to a juvenile, transfer the tool to its feet, feed the juvenile, then pick up the tool and fly off with it," Hunt wrote in the journal, *Nature.* "All current theories about the evolution of mankind rely on tool manufacture and use being central behaviors that distinguished our early ancestors from apes," said another researcher, commenting on Hunt's work. (Reuter) ...*We can thus conclude that crows are also distinguished from apes.*

Take a Whack out of Crime: The California Assembly's Public Safety Committee approved a bill allowing paddlings for juveniles convicted of graffiti. Under the measure, judges could order up to 10 strokes with a wooden paddle, which would be performed by the child's parents or a bailiff. The bill was sent to the Appropriations Committee before it comes to the floor for a vote. (AP) ...*It's more likely to get public support if they add "politician" right after "juvenile" in the bill.*

Disconnected: Asia Connect, an Internet service provider in Malaysia, proudly unveiled a new security system that owner Raymond Cheng said was impenetrable. He was so confident that he offered a $20,000 reward to anyone who could break in. It took Dinesh Nair and Thian Seong Yee just minutes to break the security and collect the reward. "I was amused by it initially, but I guess this is the price that we have to pay for doing business in the Internet," Cheng said afterward. (AP) ...*Don't whine, Ray: you set the rules.*

He Ought to Know: The state of Delaware is going ahead with an execution of a prison inmate by hanging. Billy Bailey was sentenced to hang in 1979 after being convicted of the shotgun murders of an elderly couple. In 1986, Delaware introduced death by lethal injection, and offered the alternative to anyone sentenced to hang. But Bailey kept with his original sentence. "Asking a man to choose how to die is more barbaric than hanging," he told a local newspaper. (AP) ...*Where is the shotgunning of two old people on that barbarism scale?*

Burning with Desire: A 55-year-old woman fending off a 62-year-old man in Sri Lanka found an ally in a bottle of chili sauce. "When he followed her contemplating his next move, still undressed, inflamed by his lust," panted a newspaper in Colombo, she doused him on the face and body. The man "remained several hours under water in great pain" before police arrested him for attempted rape, the paper said. (Reuter) ...*Nothing gets to a man like home cooking.*

Damn It: The Church of England has issued a new report that says Hell does exist, but it's not a burning pit of eternal torment. The fire and brimstone images in the past, they say, were just a way to terrify the masses into accepting religion, but such tactics backfire in modern times. "Christians have professed appalling theologies which made God into a sadistic monster," the report says, and the "sadistically expressed" visions of Hell have left many people with "searing psychological scars". Hell, they say now, is simply "ultimate non-being". Meanwhile, the Roman Catholic Church is sticking with the "eternal fire" concept. (Reuter) ...*Does that mean we should give up on the "streets paved with gold" at the other end of the spectrum?*

Opportunity Knocked: When his Philadelphia house caught fire, Kenneth James, 29, quickly went into action. But he wasn't working to put out the flames. Instead, when his next door neighbors rushed over to help and left their front door open, James and an accomplice burglarized their house, police say. James' sister and cousin were killed in the fire, and James has been charged with burglary, theft, criminal trespass, receiving stolen property and conspiracy. (AP) ...*Kenny: please let us know who is right, the Church of England or the Catholics.*

Got Their Man: When Missouri sheriff deputy Tony Dow was shot, a manhunt for his assailant was launched. He reported that a "scruffy looking man" shot him, but after a four-day search turned up no clues, Dow admitted he had accidentally shot himself while throwing his gun up in the air. "It was embarrassing and he knew I'd suspend or dismiss him" if he told the truth, Sheriff Fred Armes said. That might be the least of his worries: Armes is charging Dow with filing a false police report. (Reuter) ...*If only he had reported that he had been shot by an idiot, he wouldn't be in this mess.*

Just Try to Relax

Exercise Causes Major Stress for Breasts: Study

Australian AP headline

Reboot Government: According to the "Consumer Technology Attitude Survey" conducted by Techtel, one-third of Americans think that 100 computers would be more helpful in solving the country's problems than 100 politicians. On the other hand, 17 percent said sometimes they think their computer is "out to get them". (AP) ...*A number that would surely go up if we were governed by them.*

Mmm'mmm Good: The Chinese government's Ministry of Internal Trade has ordered restaurants to stop lacing winter hot pots with opium. Apparently, an economic slowdown has prompted restaurants to think of novel ways to keep customers coming back, and have taken to adding opium poppy shells to the spicy recipe. "Customers might become slightly addicted, or in any case will feel comfortable and come back again," said a spokesman for the Ministry. (Reuter) ...*Everyone else just does that with wine.*

Meet Us in the Woodshed, Senator: The state of New Hampshire is debating a bill that would allow the bare-bottomed spanking of juveniles convicted of vandalism. "Some people might say it's cruel, nasty and mean to have the sheriff paddle some kid's butt, but spanking has never done anybody a tremendous amount of harm if done properly," says the bill's sponsor, Rep. Richard Kennedy. What's good for the constituents is good for the government, Rep. Rick Trombly says: he has proposed an amendment to the bill that would also allow for the paddling of lawmakers found guilty of improper conduct. (AP) ...*Now there's an idea we can all get behind.*

Home Sweet Home: In 1992, Hamida Purivatra fled her partly completed home in Torlakovac, Bosnia-Herzgovina, as Serb troops marched in. Now, with peace, she has gotten her house back. But in her absence, a Serb carpenter had moved in and completed the structure, adding windows, doors, and a roof. "It's not really what we had planned, but it will have to do," she said, assessing the structure. "What we wanted was a third story." (Reuter) ...*Oh well, maybe next war.*

Powerballs: Connecticut's lottery commission is under fire for an advertisement run to promote its "Powerball" lotto game when the jackpot hit $87 million. "You could get even luckier than you did on prom night," the ad claimed. State lottery chief Otho Brown said he didn't notice the line when he approved the ad. "I would not have let it go through had I read further," he said. He wouldn't have had to read far: the ad was only four lines long. (AP) ...*He commonly only reads 7 out of every 51 words.*

Tickle the Ivories: MIDEM, the International Market of Records and Musical Editions in Cannes, France, is a showplace for musicians to bring their talents to the masses. One such is Candy Kane, a former stripper who is now a blues pianist. But she, of course, isn't an ordinary blues musician: she plays the piano with her breasts. "When I do this I think it destigmatizes my body," she claims. Did her previous career help? Sure, she says. "Once you pose naked in front of a crowd it gives you immense confidence." (UPI) ...*Wouldn't that depend on the response from the crowd?*

Your Meter has Expired: Former President Mathieu Kerekou of Benin parked his Boeing 747 jetliner at the airport in Ostend, Belgium. In 1989. In 1990, he was forced out of office, and the plane still sits in Belgium. Since 1989, Kerekou's plane has accumulated a parking fine of $430,000. (AP) ...*The white zone is for loading and unloading only.*

Been Down That Road: First Lady Hillary Clinton has some good advice for voters in November. "One of the reasons to keep re-electing Bill Clinton to public office, [is] to have other people drive," she says. That, she says, will help "to keep the roads safer." (Reuter) ...*On the other hand, Chelsea turns 16 next month.*

In the Bag: The Atlanta chapter of the American Red Cross had noticed the trend: blood donations dropped sharply in fiscal 1995, and the numbers didn't look any better for the first half of fiscal 1996. Action had to be taken — so they brought back the Nutter Butters. The peanut cookie, served since the 1970s to people who donated blood, was dropped in 1994 to save money. But after the cookies were replaced with another, cheaper brand, blood donations dropped, to the tune of about 20,000 pints. "I'm not sure it's a result of changing the canteen supplies," says a Red Cross spokesman, but "we'll know if we bring Nutter Butters back and donations are back up." Nabisco is helping the cause by donating 4,000 pounds of Nutter Butters. (AP) ...*And they said you couldn't squeeze blood out of corporate America.*

Stir Crazy: An unnamed 32-year-old Italian man, forced to stay home while awaiting an appeal of an armed robbery conviction, can't take the constant nagging from his mother, he said. "Put me in prison," he demanded of the local police. "I can't take it any more." Police officials refused the man's request. (Reuter) ...*All he'd have to do is clean up his room, but no. He won't listen. And you should see his friends! No good, I tell you. And did mention the time when he was six, and — did you hear a shot? I tell you, if he killed himself and made a mess in the basement....*

Especially if You Know Where They Are

Austrians Told to Stay Clear of Secret US Arsenals

Reuter headline

Scam Detector: The U.S. federal court has stopped the sale of the Quadro Positive Molecular Locator after investigators said the device didn't work. The machine consisted only of a box with an antenna, and "a small piece of polymer-coated white paper, similar to a candy bar wrapper," an FBI agent said. A $25 version of the device supposedly detected golf balls; an $8,000 version would, the manufacturer claimed, detect any substance shown on a Polaroid picture inserted into the device. As many as 1,000 of the machines were ordered by school districts and police departments for use as a drug detector. (AP) ...*The device did prove to be effective at detecting gullible school and police officials.*

Shaken, Not Stirred: A British armored vehicle ran over a land mine in Bosnia. "The crew were shaken but there were no injuries," a military spokesman reported. When an enterprising reporter asked the spokesman what the men could do to protect themselves from such incidents in the future, the unflappable spokesman offered that they could "drive more carefully". (Reuter) ...*Now you tell them.*

Sagging in the Polls: Before he was elected to the Duma (Russia's lower house of parliament), Anatoly Kashpirovsky worked as a psychic, hypnotist and faith-healer. But when he lost his seat in elections in December, Kashpirovsky refused to vacate his government-provided Moscow apartment. He says he's use his psychic powers to fight off anyone trying to evict him by rendering them impotent. Russian government officials have not yet announced what they will do about the problem. (AP) ...*Moscow needs more female cops.*

The Birds and the Bees: Southern California's Santa Ana Zoo is celebrating Valentine's Day this year by hosting the Second Annual Sex Tour. The $15 tour provides champagne to get the visitors in the mood while zoo employees explain the mating habits of various animal species. If the visitors are lucky, they see mating, but it's not guaranteed that nature will take its course during tour hours. "It's fun, it's interesting, and everyone blushes," a zoo spokeswoman says. (AP) ...*Wait until the local vice squad realizes that the zoo exhibits the animals in the nude.*

All Sales Final: Authorities in Beijing have shut down a store selling Nazi paraphernalia. The store sold replicas of Third Reich medals, uniforms and other items — "everything but weapons," a Chinese news report said. Officials at the German Embassy in Beijing were startled by the news report. "In China it's crazy," a German diplomat said. "You always have a few nuts in the U.S. and Canada, but here? It's weird." (Reuter) ...*There's even been some evidence of nuts in Germany once in a while.*

Burn Up the Road: An experimental rubber road in southeastern Washington made from ground up tires has caught fire. Apparently, rain made the tires' steel belts rust; the rusting produced enough heat to catch the rubber on fire. With the recent cold weather, "at times you can't see through the steam," said a county engineer. "It's kind of scenic." (AP) ...*I hope they can work out the problems — imagine how long concrete car tires would last.*

Road Flair: Despite living under an overpass in Novato, Calif., Neal Berry surfed the Internet, kept up with his voice mail, and answered messages to his pager. He paid for his tent, laptop computer, and the cellular phone he used to get online by holding a part-time job. "People don't understand why I chose to live on the streets, but I don't understand why they're willing to pay $500 a month just for a place to live," Berry said, explaining his budgeting choices. Berry's lifestyle came to light when he was accused of stealing the batteries used to power his computer. He denies the theft, saying he found the heavy-duty batteries. Once he gets his legal troubles behind him, Berry plans to move to Oregon to start a new career. "Not a programmer," he says. "A network specialist. They make more money." (AP) ...*Just because you're homeless doesn't mean you have to be home-pageless.*

Make a Run for the Border: U.S. Customs officers arrested a southern California man as he crossed into the state from Mexico with illegal cargo: 36 live fish being smuggled in a converted gas tank. Only 11 of the fish, all endangered garibaldi, survived to be put into quarantine at Sea World. "They seem to be in reasonably good shape," said a Sea World spokesman. "Although it's hard to tell with fish." (Portland Oregonian) ...*Then how does Sea World know its residents are in good health?*

Easy Come, Easy Go
Scientists Believe There May be Life on Mars
Reuter headline

Scientists Convinced There Was Once Life on Mars
Reuter headline, four hours later

So Far, No Mewtations: Four stray kittens found inside the San Onofre nuclear power plant in California are radioactive, plant managers say. The four, dubbed Alpha, Beta, Gamma and Neutron, apparently were contaminated by drinking radioactive water leaking from pipes. They're being cared for by plant workers, who note the contamination is dropping and the cats will soon be adopted by volunteers. A University of California cat expert said it's not unusual for felines to find ways into places where they don't belong. "The plant's security was designed to repel terrorists," he said. "Cats are not terrorists." (L.A. Times) *...But only because they have chosen not to be.*

Inside Job: Four-year-old Russell Brown of Coventry, England, was awakened by a noise in the night, and checked it out. He found some men in the house, who said they were friends of his parents. He chatted with them, and showed them the family video recorder, stereo and other valuables — even the secret place where mum hid her purse and the shed where father kept his tools. And he politely held the door while the men loaded all of it into their car and drove off. The men having left, Russell went back to bed. "We can't tell him off because he's just a four-year-old and he thought he was doing the right thing," his father said. Police are investigating the burglary. (Reuter) *...It all comes down to Childhood Rule Number 1: don't talk to strangers.*

Contempt of Court: William H. Harsha III, a judge in the 4th Ohio District Court of Appeals, was fed up, and took justice into his own hands. Not in the courtroom, but outside, where pigeons had splattered him once too often as he passed through the door. A police officer found Harsha in front of the Circleville courthouse holding a pellet rifle; two dead pigeons lay at his feet. "I just got fed up with the pigeons," the judge said later. "I shouldn't have done it." The officer charged the judge with shooting an air rifle within city limits. "The officer did the right thing," the judge said. Harsha plans to plead no contest, and could get a $250 fine and 30 days in jail. (AP) *...A harsh sentence is called for: surely a judge should know the dangers of vigilantism.*

Zapped by the Critics: A producer of a play in London is fighting critics, who say the play is "doomed", "preposterous" and in "bad taste", by offering refunds to anyone who doesn't like the show. The play is about an executioner who travels from prison to prison with his portable electric chair. "The show is not in favor of capital punishment," producer Nicholas van Hoogstraten explains. "The hero ends up in his own chair. It is a shocking, shocking scenario that is presented." (Reuter) *...Maybe more audience members would stay if they were strapped into their seats.*

As Long As You're Under Oath, We Have Some Questions: President Clinton, subpoenaed to testify in the trial of two of his Whitewater business partners, told reporters that he will comply with the order. "If they believe that something I know can help the trial, I'd be happy to cooperate," he said. (AP) *...Then surely we won't see any more delays in the Paula Jones sexual harassment lawsuit against him.*

Be My Valentine: A survey of French women found that their ideal lover is not a professional man with a good body. The survey, conducted by romance publisher Harlequin France, found only 1 percent wanted an ambitious man, only 5 percent thought that professional success was important, and just 2 percent thought a perfect body was important. What do they want, then? A man with a sense of humor was the most common response. (Reuter) *...We knew we'd be in vogue someday.*

California or Dust: Before Vic Browning died in Texas at age 83, he expressed his final wish: to take one last ride in his Cadillac

— to his nephew's crematorium in California. So Vic's son, Victor, and his grandson, Victor, dressed Vic's body up in his favorite jogging suit, strapped him in the seat, and headed west. Everything went without a hitch until they were stopped at the California border. "The officer leaned in the car, looked at my daddy and said, 'Sir, how you doing?' I said, 'Oh, he's been sleeping since we left Texas," the middle Victor said. They were waved on. "I told my daughter I wanted to keep the tradition up when I die by taking a last ride in that Corvette of hers. But Victor [III] said he's going to take me out to California on a Harley." (Reuter) ...*It'll be easy to hold on tight once rigor sets in.*

Fairway, Runway, What's the Difference? Irv Brown was golfing with friends in Boca Raton, Fla., when a small plane swept in to make an emergency landing. But they were so intent on their game, the plane had to skip the grassy fairway and hit a tree instead. "Everything would have been OK if those damn golfers would have moved," says Scott Slinko, a flying instructor in the plane with a student pilot. "We were coming down and they weren't moving, so I went for the tree." Brown wasn't apologizing. "Concentration — that's the name of the game," he said. "We were concentrating." (Reuter) ...*Besides: the pilot didn't yell "Fore!"*

Or Even the Best Way
Nobody Said Spanking Is the Only Way to Go

L.A. Times headline

Off, Off, Off, Off, Off Broadway: The City of New York has printed tourist guides for its newest attraction: Staten Island's Fresh Kills Landfill. Sanitation workers turned tour guides will follow a 30-page script to point out the various sights, such as the cranes which unload barges full of trash 24 hours a day. "There seems to be an increasing demand" for tours, insists deputy landfill director William Cloke. (AP) *...Mostly residents looking for the bullet-riddled bodies of missing relatives.*

MacGyver Squad: U.S. troops in Bosnia-Herzegovina are apparently bored. Enterprising grunts have taken to using the chemical heating packs that come with their "Meals, Ready-to-Eat" to make small explosive devices to perk up their days. MREs are coming to be known as "Meals, Ready-to-Explode". (Reuter) *...Considering Army food, wouldn't this be considered a biological weapon?*

His Own Image: A San Rafael, Calif., man who had his name changed to Ubiquitous Perpetuity God has been convicted of indecent exposure and sentenced to nine months in jail. God, 68, who has been convicted 18 times for similar acts since 1978, came to the U.S. from Cuba in search of "women, silver, gold, knowledge and God." God said he exposes himself to women so they "could have some type of awareness of God." (AP) *...And it works: when they see him, they scream "Oh My God!"*

The Party of the First Part: Rex and Teresa LeGalley have everything covered. The Albuquerque, N.M., couple signed a 16-page prenuptial agreement that dictates everything from the brand of gas they'll put in their car to the time they go to bed and get up. "A lot of people say a prenuptial is something you do in case you get divorced," said Teresa (who has been married once before). Instead, they plan to use it to ensure they don't get one. "This gives us a list we can live with," said Rex (who's been married twice before). (AP) *...Sure Rex can live with it: he has a signed contract for sex 3–5 times a week.*

Urban Darwinism: Robert Phillips was pretty sure the two teenaged carjackers who were making him drive his sports car to his Tallahassee, Fla., bank at gunpoint were going to kill him when they were through draining his account. So before they could, he swerved his car and crashed into a parked truck. Phillips escaped injury thanks to an air bag. One carjacker was killed in the crash; the other had to be cut from the wreckage, but suffered only minor injuries. He now faces kidnapping and carjacking charges. Phillips isn't terribly upset with the death. "They were intent on removing me from the equation," he said. (AP) ...*Obviously, they flunked algebra.*

Urban Darwinism II: "He ran outside and said, 'Whoops'," says Cadiz, Ky., police chief Ray White. A gunman robbed a food mart of $170, then fled to his getaway car parked out front. It was locked, its keys in the ignition. With the store clerks calling the cops, Kevin Stanley Stokes, 25, frantically kicked through the back window of the car so he could get inside — just as police arrived. He led officers on a 21-mile chase before giving up. (AP) ...*How much would you bet that the passenger-side door was unlocked?*

Urban Darwinism III: "He missed the beeper number by one number," says an Omaha, Neb., police spokesman. A man was paging a customer, and accidentally misdialed, reaching instead the pager of an undercover narcotics officer, who called the number on his beeper. "The guy indicated he was a drug dealer and that he sold large amounts of crack cocaine," the spokesman said. The officer played along, met the man and purchased more than an ounce of crack. The dealer and an accomplice have been arrested. (AP) ...*Police are still awaiting a call from the guy with the other pager.*

If the Smell Won't Emit You Must Acquit: Villagers in the British town of Bruntingthorpe are so distressed over uncurbed dogs that they are taking stool samples from all the pooches in town to create a DNA data base so that ...*uh*... evidence from canine squat-and-runs can be identified. Will dog owners cooperate with the data collection? "I am sure they will all be happy to take part, if only to prove their innocence," said Parish councillor Ian Eperon. (Reuter) ...*And, once cleared, they can then hunt for the "real" poopers.*

Shoreline Property Values Skyrocket: Brazilian congressman Fernando Gabeira has introduced a constitutional amendment to legalize nudity on all beaches in that country; currently, only five beaches are "officially" clothing-optional. But Rep. Gerson Peres thinks the new freedom "will start a vicious circle. People who go nude on the beach will soon want to walk around naked everywhere." (AP) ...*So what's your point?*

With Friends Like These: It's pretty typical for the president to be bashed by the opposing party. But Bill Clinton has to contend with sniping by his own partisans, too. "Clinton's an unusually good liar. Unusually good. Do you realize that?" asked Democrat Sen. Bob Kerrey in a magazine interview. Democrat Sen. Ernest Hollings notes that Clinton's approval polls are getting better — "If they get up to 60 percent, his people tell me Bill can start dating again," Hollings told a newspaper. Hollings said he was joking, and Kerry apologized to Clinton. But when asked if he really thinks Clinton is a liar, Kerry simply said "I don't really want to comment further." (AP) ...*Indeed: who needs to?*

Ma-Ma: Authorities in Stamford, Conn., were relieved to find that a body they found was not a dead baby, but a plastic doll. The 11-inch baby with a severed arm was found in a drainage ditch; police called for the medical examiner, who declared it dead and sent it for autopsy. The chief medical examiner figured it all out, and dismissed criticism, calling it a case of better safe than sorry. A police spokesman defended officers at the scene. "It wasn't like it had yellow hair... and a belly button that squeaks," he said. (AP) ...*No, but how many newborns have they seen with two glass eyes?*

Antisocial, Not Uncivilized
Burglars Take Tea Break During Robbery
Reuter headline

Fashion Police: Costa Mesa, Calif., police have launched a new tactic in their war on local prostitutes: when arrested, their clothes are impounded. "There's a certain manner of dress that's designed to attract attention," a police spokesman explained. When released, the women are given paper jumpsuits to wear. Officers hope the time it takes them to change back into street clothes — and the money it will cost them — will slow them down before they can get back on the street for more soliciting. (AP) ...*Maybe, but you'd think it would be even easier to undress when only wearing paper.*

Fashion Police II: Henry Holmes was shocked when he went to visit his six-year-old son at a private kindergarten: he found Gerald wearing a dress, playing house. "One of those long white silk dresses with sequins in it," Holmes said. He removed the boy from the Baltimore, Md., school, and enrolled him in public school. Teachers say the dress was the boy's choice. (AP) ...*It's shocking the things they teach kids these days! Sequins? Before sundown?*

Come In, It's Open: When a car belonging to the British Royal Family's protection squad was stolen, police weren't worried too much about the car. It was the keys to Windsor Castle they were concerned with. And the score of security passes. And a police-man's uniform. And the telephone numbers of all the lines in Buckingham Palace. "It was an act of extreme stupidity to have left these things in the car," a police spokesman said. (Reuter) ...*With all the goings on with the family lately, the queen would probably just as soon the locks be changed anyway.*

Flipped the Bird: Roscoe Crawford of Jonesboro, Ga., came home from church with his wife to find that a bird had flown into his daughter's bedroom. He tried to get it out, but the bird "attacked" him. So he went and got his 9mm pistol and shot the bird dead. But the bullet didn't stop there. It went through the wall, through the dining room and into the kitchen, where Crawford's wife Rita was doing the dishes. It skipped off the top of her head, causing minor injury, then headed outside. Police did not charge Crawford with any crime, but granted his request that they take his gun away from him. (AP) ...*Wasn't that more likely Rita's request?*

Their Kidneys Said it Looked Familiar: The first World Confer-ence on Auto-Urine Therapy was held in Goa, India, this weekend for 600 delegates from 17 nations exploring the medical benefits of drinking your own urine. "It gives me and my wife tremendous energy and stamina," claims the former chief of India's navy. G.K. Thakkar, president of the event's host, the Water of Life

Foundation, said drinking urine cured him of dysentery and eczema, and made him a "bold orator". Also, he says, urine is a good cure for tooth and eye problems. (Reuter) ... *What does it do for bad breath?*

Cop Dusters: Police in Walnut Park, Calif., were chasing a car when one of the occupants started throwing out handfuls of white powder. As the cops closed in, the volume went up, until a cardboard box full of powder was tossed overboard. After four blocks, the car was stopped and the two occupants arrested on investigation of dealing cocaine. Police and streetsweepers gathered up more than two pounds of the powder as evidence. (AP) *...I'd never use cocaine, but I have to admit I'm curious as to what it smells like.*

Free Sample: "Three or four very unusual circumstances" combined at the offices of Cable TV Arlington (Virginia), resulting in erotic movies being shown unscrambled on a cable TV channel for several hours. "There was a computer malfunction," a spokesman explained, adding that further safeguards were being put in place to prevent the error from repeating. Complaints? Only 11 of 60,000 customers called the company about the problem, but they weren't necessarily angry. "Most just wanted to be sure they wouldn't get charged for it," the spokesman said. (Reuter) *...Mainly because they had already seen them.*

Clear the Air: When the Ku Klux Klan burned a cross in Modesto, Calif., local police said they couldn't do anything because it was done on the private property of the Imperial Wizard. But the San Joaquin Valley Unified Air Pollution Control District says it can do something: it plans to file court papers asking for a $50,000 fine from the Klan for polluting the air, plus an injunction against future cross burnings. "They are doing it as a get-in-our-face kind of thing," a pollution control attorney said, adding that only agricultural materials can be burned, not crosses. (AP) *...Is this really what locals meant when they asked for a stop to the Klan's "vile emissions"?*

Have You Seen This Airport? City officials in Denver, Colo., are considering putting the telephone number for the Denver International Airport on milk cartons because the airport's number was omitted from the new telephone directory. "It's very frustrating for travelers or consumers who want to reach the airport and they can't," an airport spokesman said. "God, are we missing?" a city councilwoman asked. "Put out a reward." (AP) ...*As if anyone would answer anyway.*

A Penny for your Thoughts: An unidentified Frenchman was a bit peeved about having to pay taxes on his gambling winnings — the bill came to 3,730,606 francs. So he paid the levy in one-franc coins, delivered to the tax collector in Viarmes by three armored trucks. "The franc is the monetary unit of France," the man said simply. Tax collectors didn't have a problem with the payment. "We greeted him with a smile," a spokeswoman said. "He paid his taxes on time." (Reuter) ...*I'd be worried about that smile. Can you say "audit three years in a row"?*

It Can Happen Just That Fast

168 Goats Roam
Los Angeles Freeway

AP headline

---

168 Goats Killed In Accident

AP headline, two minutes later

Toenailed: Bonnie Booth, 38, of Muncie, Ind., tried to remove a callus on her toe using a razor blade. "It didn't work," a police spokesman said. "She was afraid it was getting infected because it hurt real bad." Time for a doctor? Not for Booth: she switched from the razor to her .410-gauge shotgun. Anesthetic? "She told investigators she drank a gallon of vodka and two or three beers," police said. Booth was taken to a hospital for psychiatric evaluation. No word on the efficacy of her self-surgery. (AP) ...*Before now, she was known for shooting her mouth off when she drank.*

Good Girls Don't: A 55-year-old man in Burbank, Calif., put an ad in a sex magazine catering to sadomasochists, and was happy when a woman responded to his offer of a blind date. When she arrived at his home, he allowed her to strip him, handcuff him, and strap him to a proctology table he had in his "playroom". Then she put a hood over his head and *really* went to work: she and an accomplice robbed the house. The man wasn't found until the next day, when the mailman heard him calling for help. (Burbank Leader) *...That was fantastic! Are you free on Friday night?*

Good Girls Don't II: It was an interesting week in Burbank. Salle Dumm, 51, has been accused of unlawful intercourse and contributing to the delinquency of a minor after an incident with a 17-year-old Burbank High School football player at her home. He says Dumm, the president of the Burbank Education Foundation, told him to come to her room, where he found her nude on the bed. "Do this for your team. I can help out your team financially," she said, according to court testimony. The affair lasted no more than seven minutes. Apparently, however, she didn't come through with any cash. "I haven't seen it," says Willard Williams, the school's principal. "If I had, I'd be out there putting up new bleachers." (AP) *...Don't blame the kid, Willard. He wasn't sure if you'd accept a check.*

Health Food: Ibama, Brazil's environmental protection institute, is seeking a ban of beer advertising which uses chimpanzees as actors. The primates are often seen, for instance, driving cars in the ads, or having drinks with bikini-clad women. "Driving a car and drinking beer or soda is not a monkey's natural habitat," says an Ibama spokeswoman. (Reuter) *...Quite: they are known to prefer banana daiquiris.*

Army-Navy Game: "The Army told her that we couldn't guarantee her training for a job in intelligence like we had said. One of our people went over and told the Army recruiter that 'yes, we could'," said Navy recruiter James Hutchins. The Navy recruitment office in Leesburg, Fla., is next door to the Army recruitment office. The Army recruiters didn't like the friendly competition: three Army recruiters came over to explain their case to the Navy. They came armed with a crowbar, and two marines were injured in the ruckus. The woman signed up with the Navy. "She said she wasn't too impressed with the Army," Hutchins said. Two of the Army recruiters were charged with battery, the other with aggravated battery. (AP) ...*They can beat up more people by 10:00 am than most people beat up all day.*

Occupational Hazard: Two teen-aged robbers in Miami got a little carried away when they attempted to hold up a grocery store. The 18-year-old accidentally fired his gun, hitting his 16-year-old accomplice in the leg. The surprise and pain caused him to tightly grip his gun and it too went off — hitting the first robber in the leg. "I've had robbers shoot themselves before, but I never had two robbers shoot each other," a police detective said after the two were arrested. "I knew there was a mistake," said store clerk Aijaz Rizva. "They were the only ones bleeding." (Reuter) ...*Surely that was preferable to him.*

Ghost Stories: First-year Yale medical student Christopher Wahl heard the stories in the dorm just like all the first-year students had for years. A spooky legend about hundreds of brains stored in bottles in the dorm's basement. But unlike the thousands that came before him, Wahl decided to check — and found the stories were true. "I could just see telling my parents I got thrown out of medical school for this," Wahl remembers. But "no one really asked, 'What were you doing skulking around the bottom of the dorm?'" The archives contained not only brains, but photographs and 50,000 pages of records of Dr. Harvey Cushing, a pioneer in neurosurgery at Harvard who finished his career at Yale. Wahl took a year off to catalog the extensive find; Cushing died in 1939. "It's fun for me just because there are generations of physicians who never knew the brains were down there," Wahl said. (AP) ...*I can see the headline in the Harvard Crimson now: "Yalies Claim They Didn't Know They Had Brains".*

Don't Wait Up: Hong Kong's Cheung Han Son-mei agreed to babysit an 11-month-old baby for three months, and was paid HK$9,000 in advance. He's apparently a good little boy: "I would happily take care of him for life," Cheung says. She may have to:

the mother has not come back for the boy, and it's been four years now. Police are searching for the mother. (Reuter) ...*Even without a raise, by the time the kid's 18, the mother will owe her HK$606,000.*

Best Two-out-of-Three?
Coin-toss Used to Choose Spouse
Reuter headline

Hugh Grant Syndrome: Florida state representative Marvin Couch, part of the self-proclaimed "Capitol God Squad", has resigned from office after Tallahassee vice squad officers caught him ...*um*... employing a prostitute in his car. Both Couch and the prostitute were arrested. The married Couch, 42, who had received a "perfect" rating from the Christian Coalition of Florida, admitted it was not the first time he had purchased services from prostitutes. Officers approached the car, parked at noon in a shopping center parking lot in full view of passers-by, and had no trouble figuring out what was going on inside. "If it were a fire, they would be fully involved," a police spokesman said. (AP) ...*Perhaps that explains why the cops wanted to squirt them with a hose.*

Peter, Panned: When the West Yorkshire Playhouse in Leeds, England, wouldn't refund their money, Amanda and Mark Mitchener felt they had only one recourse: they sued the Playhouse. It seems their three-year-old son, Morris, was frightened by the production of "Peter Pan". "Morris was terrified from the moment the lights went down and the narrator started speaking," Amanda insists. "It was like an X-rated horror movie for a child of his age." A Playhouse spokesman begs to differ. "We tried to remain faithful to the original play," he said. "We've had heaps of praise from children and grandchildren." (Reuter) ... *"Every time a child says, 'I don't believe in fairies,' there is a fairy somewhere that falls down dead." —Peter (Act 1).*

Juvenile Court II: A Boston judge has granted a restraining order barring Jonathan Inge, 3, from making Stacy Pevnev, also 3, cry — indeed, Judge Charles Spurlock ruled the two must play separately in the park. Stacy's mother said she wouldn't have gone to court if Mrs. Inge had simply apologized for an incident where Jonathan kicked Stacy, but instead "she applauds and encourages Jonathan to be violent, to fight and kick." Jonathan's attorney, Howard Speicher, was a bit more philosophical. "Maybe it's a sign, and this is coming from a lawyer, of how people are starting to rely too much on the courts to solve problems that just don't belong there," he said after the order was granted. (AP) *..."Maybe," Howard? What do you need, bolts of lightning? Superlawyer F. Lee Bailey in jail? What?*

Tireless Justice: Dale Tippins, currently serving 18 years in prison, was granted a new trial because his lawyer slept through his 1986 trial on drug charges. "The evidence ... demonstrates that counsel was unconscious for numerous extended periods of time during which the defendant's interests were at stake," ruled the 2nd U.S. Court of Appeals in New York. Even "the court reporter heard him snore a couple of times." A juror estimated defense attorney Louis Tirelli was asleep through two-thirds of the trial. The court, however, was careful to limit its ruling, noting that convictions shouldn't be thrown out for simple cases of defense sleepiness, lest lawyers fake sleeping to provide later grounds for appeal. (AP) *...What do sleeping lawyers dream of?*

Sign Here: Simon Alciere was surprised when his Amherst, Mass., company, Simon's Stamps, was recently awarded a federal contract, since nearly two years had gone by since he submitted his bid, "a few hundred pages of paperwork". The government contract, for about 40,000 rubber stamps a year, will triple his business. But the paperwork hasn't stopped. "Today I promised never to incorporate any munitions made in South Africa in my rubber stamps, and to be a drug-free work place if we ever employ as many as 50 people," Alciere said. (AP) *...Next time, include a rubber stamp that says "Approved" when you submit a bid. It'll help speed things up.*

Star Dreck: Paramount Pictures has filed suit against a Salt Lake City theater group, charging the 200-seat theater's "Star Twek" parody infringes on the studio's "Star Trek" copyrights and trademarks. The parody follows captain "James T. Smirk" and his pointy-eared first officer "Mr. Schlock" as they face their greatest challenge — the "corporate downsizing" that follows intergalactic peace. The suit says "irreparable injury" will come to the 30-year-old Trek franchise if the court doesn't order a stop to it. (AP) *...Paramount shouldn't sue; they should send their writers over for some fresh ideas.*

Altered, Dot, Reality: President Bill Clinton and V.P. Al Gore joined 20,000 volunteers in an effort to wire 3,000 California public schools to the Internet. Clinton wants all schools to join the White House on the Net so kids can tap into the vast resources offered online. "What's our e-mail address, Al?," Clinton asked. "It's www dot whitehouse, one word, don't capitalize it, dot, 1600 Pennsylvania Avenue," Gore replied, completely botching their actual addresses — "president@whitehouse.gov" and "vicepresident@whitehouse.gov". (AP) *...No wonder Bill and Al never answer their e-mail: they're waiting for it to be dropped into the metal box at the front gate.*

Bad Dog! Bad!
Police Hold Dog After Bank Robbery
Reuter headline

Bye, Bye Birdies: Scotland Yard is investigating reports of thefts from London's Trafalgar Square. It's not the monuments that are at risk, but the pigeons — locals say two men have taken at least 1,000 pigeons away in boxes in recent months. Police think the birds are ending up on restaurant tables. Locals are worried the diminishing bird population will cut down on the tourist trade. According to Bernard Rayner, who sells bird seed to the tourists to feed the birds, "Trafalgar Square is the only place in the country you can get a wild animal to sit on your head." (AP) ...*Which is exactly why some tourists refuse to go there.*

Can I Get You Anything? Police in St. Petersburg, Fla., were surprised when a handcuffed shoplifting suspect they had brought to the station jumped into a patrol car and drove off. Officers decided not to chase after him — "We just didn't feel there was a need to endanger the public over something like this," a police spokesman said. The car was found 100 blocks away a few hours later. But Anastasios Balodimas, 29, was free less than 24 hours. He was arrested the next day, as the suspect in another shoplifting case. He was charged with grand theft and resisting arrest. (AP) ...*Can't blame him too much — he still needed a few things.*

Two-Time Loser II: Vincent Santana, in a Los Angeles jail on charges of lewd conduct and making obscene phone calls, was found to be using a public phone in the jail to make harassing phone calls. Police say the calls started within days of Santana's incarceration, and as many as 200 calls were made from the jail phone in the last several months. (Pasadena Star-News) ...*Where did he get all the quarters?*

Vacation Scenery: Two American men vacationing in the Czech Republic fought with an armed intruder in the apartment where they were staying. Frank Pond, 46, of Chicago and Don Royse, 63, of St. Louis tackled the man and tried to knock him unconscious with the butt of his gun. When that was unsuccessful, the two sat on him until police arrived to take care of the matter. It turns out the man was Ladislav Winkelbauer, the country's most wanted man after his escape from prison. "It's a vacation we'll never forget," Royse said. "I've never seen a gun that closely before." (Reuter) ...*The Czechs probably had a hard time believing there are American men who have never handled guns before.*

You May Already Be a Winner: Four Chicago men by the name of Eric Thompson are upset with a local adoption agency over a letter each received. "You have been named as the father of an unborn baby," each letter said, and "the law requires that the agency make diligent efforts to locate and notify the child's father" of the baby's pending adoption. At least one of the men opened the letter in front of his wife. "All I could say was, 'I don't know what this is. Honest.' Well, what do you think a wife thinks when she hears that?" The Children's Home and Aid Society is "rethinking its strategy" in such cases, and admits such letters have been sent to as many as 60 men with a common name. In the recent case, none of the four Eric Thompsons was the 19-year-old father being sought. (AP) ...*If Mr. Thompson thinks he had a hard time explaining to his wife, he should talk to Father Thompson at St. Mary's.*

Poster Girl: Marina Ripa di Meana, an Italian marchioness who likes to go out on a limb in support of liberal causes, was previously known for putting up a banner at a party last summer at the French embassy protesting France's nuclear bomb testing. Now, she has posed for a billboard for the Italian International Animal Welfare Fund to campaign against using animals for fur. The advertisement shows the 52-year-old in a full-frontal nude pose; the caption by her pubic hair notes that it is "The only fur I'm not ashamed to wear." (Reuter) ...*The tough part is putting it in cold storage for the summer.*

Beam Her Up: Barbara Adams has been dismissed as an alternate juror in the Whitewater fraud trial in Little Rock, Ark. She violated the judge's gag order and talked to the media — not about the case, but about her daily attire: a Star Trek uniform, complete with phaser, tricorder and communicator. She says she wants to promote the TV show and its ideals of inclusion, tolerance and peace. "If it helps to make people think a little bit more what those ideals are, then I'll keep wearing this uniform," she said. (AP) ...*People wear baseball caps every day, but they probably don't inspire others to make $30 million per year playing ball.*

Whole Lotto Trouble: Phillip W. Cappella won $2.7 million playing the lottery in 1985. On his tax return that year, he claimed $65,000 in gambling losses against his winnings, saving over $20,000 in federal taxes. Suspicious auditors asked for proof of those losses, so Cappella produced 200,000 losing scratch-off lottery tickets. Auditors were not convinced: that would mean

Cappella would have had to scratch off nearly 550 tickets a day, every day, to accumulate that many tickets. Investigators allege the 200,000 losing tickets were rented for the audit for $500; Cappella and his tax preparer now face conspiracy charges. (AP) *...The only things you can count on life are death, taxes, and people trying to cheat on both.*

Life After Death
California Recalls Own Massacre
AP headline

Don't Worry, Yuri, the Housekeeper Arrives Tomorrow: American astronaut Shannon Lucid, the first woman to go into space five times, has arrived at Russia's *Mir* space station to start a five-month stint working on scientific experiments. "I think it'll be a great adventure," she said before launch. Were the Russians looking forward to having a woman on the station for so long? Last week, Gen. Yuri Glazkov, the deputy commander of the Gagarin Cosmonaut Training Center, said yes, it would indeed be nice to have her there, "because we know that women love to clean." (AP) *...The good news: no underwear on the floor. The bad news: it floats.*

Attractive Nuisance: Residents of the posh southern California town of San Marino are concerned about crime. But city leaders don't want the security bars being installed on some homes to impact property values. "They detract from the ambiance of the neighborhood," sniffs the police chief. The mayor notes it's one thing for a Spanish-style house, which typically has ironwork already, to have bars, but another for a ranch-style house to have them. The City Council, therefore, has passed the "bar and grille" ordinance, requiring homeowners to submit plans for city approval before they can install security bars. Plans will be reviewed by the Design Review Committee to ensure installations are safe — and attractive. (Pasadena Star-News) *...Well, Marge, the installation is approved, as long as they're mauve.*

Bars and Stripes Forever: Jailers in Britain are upset that prison uniform shirts are becoming a fashion item. The striped shirts, which sell for as much as 50 pounds on the black market, are valued for their unique style and rarity. "People who wear it want others to think they have been inside," says one trader. "People pay for the label. The prison crown is as valuable as Calvin Klein." (Reuter) ...*A lot of people want Calvin Klein to wear those shirts himself.*

Food Kills: When a Hungarian woman getting something to eat leaned into a sauerkraut barrel at a relative's home near Ebes, outside Budapest, she was overcome by the contents' fumes, passed out, fell into the barrel and drowned in the 12 inches of cabbage juice inside. Meanwhile, a young Moslem girl died in France from eating a liver-kebab, made from a sheep that was later found to have anthrax. (AP, Reuter) ...*I told my father stories like this when I was a kid, trying to avoid his experimental meals. Nice to finally have proof I was right.*

Kids' TV Wars: A 21-year-old man claiming to be armed with a bomb took a radio station manager hostage in Wanganui, New Zealand, and demanded that the station play "The Rainbow Connection", a song performed by the Muppets, for 12 hours to "tell people how he felt." And in Australia, Parliament has agreed to reschedule its popular daily Question Time television show, where Members are allowed to question the Prime Minister and other cabinet members, so it doesn't clash in the daytime schedule with another popular show — Sesame Street. (AP, 2) ...*Handy guide: the show with the screaming children probably isn't Sesame Street.*

Let Me Get a Pen: Robert Shields, 77, of Dayton, Wash., is the author of perhaps the longest personal diary in history. His recordings of his daily events — all of them, including his trips to the bathroom — was started in 1972 and now stretches to 37.5 million words. Since having a stroke in 1991, his output has slowed to a mere 1 million words per year, but he still manages to transcribe his daily jottings on a typewriter, a task that takes about four hours a day. July 25, 1993, 7 a.m.: "I cleaned out the tub and scraped my feet with my fingernails to remove layers of dead skin." Jan. 27, 1994, 9:55 a.m.: "Jim Broatch of Milford, Conn., called ... he is head of some sort of organization that deals with compulsion and I admitted the diary was 'an obsession of sorts.' He is sending me free literature about the organization." Shields isn't recording his life to aid future historians. Rather, "you might say I'm a nut," he says simply. (AP) ...*This could end up in some sort of freakish Warhol loop: he'll be writing about people who write about his writings.*

Smile: Some say Britain has more security cameras per capita than any other country. Now, an enterprising British company is buying up as many security camera tapes it can find and marketing copies of excerpts. "Caught in the Act" shows couples having sex in unlikely locations, people using department store changing rooms, robberies, and drug dealers fighting each other. Parliament is outraged, which has helped sales. "We sold 60,000 in the first morning" after Parliament objected to the first tape, James Hunt, one of the video's "researchers", said. "We've ordered another 125,000 copies." A sequel, "Really Caught in the Act", prompted more complaints from Parliament, making Hunt gleeful at the publicity. "We're hoping we can keep this [controversy] going," Hunt says. (Washington Post) ...*Parliament knows it's just a matter of time before some Members are featured in a tape.*

At Least, a Big Chunk of It
Oil Barge Breaks Off Texas
AP headline

Fast Talker: "Well, you got your Whopper's worth," a murder suspect told Miami police. He had just confessed to the killing between bites of the police-bought hamburger. But he left out the ending — "I'm really hungry. Buy me a cheese steak," he urged. When detectives complied, he finished his confession — adding an admission that he also committed a couple of robberies. Suspects so much prefer fast food to jailhouse fare that "we should open an account at Burger King," said Miami homicide detective Kent Hart. (AP) *...I foresee a future lawsuit over "cruel and unusual" treatment coming out of this.*

Relief Effort: A cruise ship passenger recovering from a bout of drinking had an urgent need, so he climbed over a railing to urinate into the ocean. But the passenger, an unidentified man is his 20s, managed to fall overboard during the maneuver, dropping 75 feet into the Atlantic off San Juan, Puerto Rico. He survived by swimming four miles to shore. The ship, "Celebration", resumed its itinerary once it learned he was safe. (Reuter) *...There's nothing like a little swim to sober you up.*

Cover That Microphone! Internal Revenue Service employee Howard A. Baltazar, 42, was caught in an Oakland, Calif., athletic club's locker room with a video camera hidden in his gym bag. The confiscated tape shows three trips to the locker room, where a number of men can be seen showering and changing clothes. But police couldn't figure out what, if anything, they could charge him with. "It's not a lewd act, it's not involving a juvenile, it's not involving this guy selling a tape, and he wasn't trespassing," an Oakland police investigator said. The state's Peeping Tom law didn't apply, because the tape was not shot through a door or window. Police finally figured out they could charge three misdemeanor counts of "recording confidential conversations" since the tape has a soundtrack of the mens' locker room discussions. The IRS is conducting its own investigation. (AP) *...Just trying to get some stock tips, that's all.*

A Modest Proposal: Much of Britain's cattle population may be infected with the dreaded "mad cow" disease, and all of them may have to be destroyed. But Cambodia has a better idea of what to do with them. "The English have 11 million mad cows and Cambodia has roughly the same number of equally mad land mines," a newspaper in Phnom Penh said. The cattle should be sent out to roam the countryside and trip the mines before people step on them, the paper said. "The plan is simple, practical, and will make mincemeat of the problem overnight." (Reuter) *..."What passing-bells for these who die as cattle? Only the* *monstrous anger of the guns."* —*Wilfred Owen (1893-1918), British poet.*

Collared by the Cops: Brett Donohoe found a stray dog at an Uhrichsville, Ohio, shopping center, and decided to take it home. He put it in his pickup truck, then stepped away to do an errand. But when he got back, the truck was gone. Meanwhile, patrolman James Myers spotted the pickup as it pulled out of the shopping center parking lot, noticing it weaving around as it went down the road. Thinking the driver was drunk, Myers chased after it. The truck drove through a yard and two fields before crashing. No people were inside; the stray dog Donohoe had found was behind the wheel. Donohoe was charged with leaving his vehicle unattended with the engine running. The dog was apparently not charged. (AP) *...No one wanted to smell its breath to see if it was drunk.*

Impure: Kellogg is recalling boxes of Frosted Flakes cereal from stores in six states because they're "contaminated". With what? Kellogg's Cocoa Krispies cereal. (UPI) *...But check before you return them: if they're just "rat pellets", they're not covered by the recall.*

Sorry, We're Out of Babycakes Today: "She's wonderful," said one Capitol Hill staffer. "She's just a burst of sunshine, a friendly, wonderful, lovely woman," agreed a Senate aide. But Christopher Held, an aide to a Kentucky senator, complained that Bernice Harris, 58, a Capitol coffee shop employee, had sexually harassed him by calling him "baby". For the past 30 years, Harris has called most everyone she meets "baby", "babycakes", "sugar", or something similar. Harris was transferred after the complaint, but an outcry by other staffers got her reinstated to her former job. (AP) *...She had a good defense: Held was indeed acting like a baby.*

Inside Job: The janitor was suspicious: it seemed that every time Dennis Ferriter, 57, ate his lunch in the school's supply room, a roll of toilet paper ended up missing. He even noticed that when Ferriter, the principal of Tri-County High School in Plainfield, Wis., was absent for a day, a roll did *not* disappear. Police searched Ferriter's car after lunch one day, and found a roll of toilet paper. It was easy to trace it to the school supply: police had marked the rolls with invisible ink. Ferriter has been suspended; the district attorney is deciding whether it should bother to file charges. (AP) ...*They don't need to: the kids will never let him forget.*

Merry Men: Nottingham First, a consortium of businessmen in the English town best known for Robin Hood, is trying to come up with a new symbol for the town — they prefer an image that is less "hostile" to businesses and investors. "A man who robbed the rich to give to the poor. That is rather out of fashion these days," a spokesman said. (Reuter) ...*What, they've never heard of Democrats?*

Though They're Not Necessarily Afterward

Sane People May See Angels, Ghosts — Report

Reuter headline

Wanna Be Near Bill: Joe Craig Fancher, 44, was arrested after he drove onto a closed freeway in Oklahoma City and attempted to join President Clinton's passing motorcade. He was charged with driving under the influence, possession of marijuana, and "interrupting a motorcade". A few days before, an "extremely intoxicated" marine was arrested after trying to climb over the fence at the White House. Cpl. Jebediah Morris, 21, said he thought the brightly lit compound behind the fence was the Quantico marine base in Virginia. (AP, 2) ...*Trust us, son. The commander here isn't a marine.*

In Search of the Obvious: Howard Kahn, a lecturer at Edinburgh's Heriot Watt University, has studied the matter intently, and says he's figured out why Scottish soccer teams can't seem to win World Cup and other competitions: they're not good players. "Managers and coaches need to spend more time with their players, teaching skills and ability," Kahn told the Edinburgh

International Science Festival. (Reuter) ...*Huh. I thought it was because they made fewer goals than their opponents.*

Nothing but Net: A 32-foot-high portrait of Chicago Bulls basketballer Dennis Rodman is causing traffic tie-ups in downtown Chicago, as people stop to gape at the player looking down at traffic. Bigsby & Kruthers, a clothing store, recently added Rodman next to a similar-sized portrait of Michael Jordan, which has been on the wall for years without causing a problem. The Chicago Sun-Times suggests the attention-catching portrait be replaced with someone less "compelling or mesmerizing" — such as the governor, who is "so boring that's not going to cause any traffic tie-ups," columnist Richard Roeper says. (UPI) ...*Motorists are simply watching to see if the Rodman portrait head-butts the Jordan portrait.*

School Daze: Thomas Mealey, a Uinta County (Wyo.) judge, was tired of seeing juveniles go from petty crimes to a career of lawbreaking. So when a 14-year-old came before him after crashing a car in a drunken joyride, he decided to try an experiment. Rather than giving the typical probation, he sentenced the teen to six months in the county jail. If he chooses, the boy can get out each day to go to school. "Wisely, he elected to go to school," Mealey said. After school, it's right back to jail, where he's kept away from adult prisoners. "He's got a lot of study time," the local sheriff says. Jailers are helping the boy with his homework and serving as positive role models. "It's my understanding he gets As and Bs now," the sheriff added. (AP) ...*Sounds like a great idea, but some parent will be inspired by it and get into trouble for doing the same thing.*

School Daze II: "When we told Nick the plan, he kind of went into shock," says Mark Rademacher. Nick, 17, was failing all of his classes at Greeley (Colo.) West High School, and his parents didn't know what to do. So they accepted the offer from Rev. Dave Mundy, the pastor of Greeley Missionary Baptist Church: in exchange for $1.50 per day to pay for his lunch, Mundy is following Nick to classes to make sure he goes to school. During classes, Mundy sits a few desks away, working on his Sunday sermons. "I know Nick can outrun me, but when I catch him I will use these," Mundy says, holding up a pair of handcuffs left over from his previous profession as a police officer. (AP) ...*Wonder if the kid would prefer jail?*

Milk the Farmers: Two sculptors in Manchester, England, feel sorry for farmers who may have to destroy their cattle in the "mad cow" crisis sweeping the country. "We're worried that it's going to leave the countryside looking desolate," says Chris Gilmore, so he and partner Paul Meedham plan to provide farmers life-sized cardboard cows to set in their fields "to fill the gaps." The cardboard bovines are blank so Gilmore and Meedham can "paint on demand" to mimic any breed. Gilmore's prototype is for sale for 250 pounds. (UPI) ...*My steak looks great, but it tastes awful!*

I Call This One "Mice Got-Hard": A fine arts senior at the University of Florida has been charged with cruelty to animals after he used mice for an art project. Vincent Gothard, 25, allegedly dipped live mice into liquid polyester resin. After it hardened, he cut it into two-inch blocks — some containing mice, some "pieces of mice" — for use in a sculpture and a mobile. "My only response is, so what? They are feeder mice," said Robert Rush, Gothard's lawyer. "If their allegation is true ...they died instantly once they hit the vat. Is that any different than killing them in a mouse trap?" Also, he says, the animal cruelty statute is too broad. "Does that include a lobster that is dropped into boiling water alive?" If convicted, Gothard faces up to five years in prison and a $10,000 fine. (AP) ...*If not convicted, he faces his teacher and Florida art critics.*

Pen Pal: Manuel Pardo Jr. is slick. He puts ads in newspapers saying he seeks a "real-honest relationship", and he finds them. Actually, though, what he wants a relationship with is the women's money — 26 women have sent Pardo money since January 1995. Pardo, 39, is in prison in Florida for the murder of nine people. "I could kick myself, but I've learned one thing — there are a lot of diabolical people out there," one woman said after she realized she was just one of many who had sent Pardo money. (AP) ...*Hint, sweetheart: a lot of the people in prison are* *diabolical. That's why they're there.*

Lawsuits 'R' Us: A Sunrise, Fla., police officer is suing a woman he saved because he was injured in the incident. Jane Liberatore was facing her husband, Anthony, who had a shotgun and planned to kill her; he had just shot and killed her boyfriend, police say. Sgt. Mark Byers smashed through a window to save her life, but sliced open his hand in the process. The cop's attorney says the injury is partly Mrs. Liberatore's fault. "When you cheat on your husband and create the potential for murder or aggravated assault and a police officer is injured as a result, you make your own bed and you have to sleep in it," attorney Charles Morehead explained. (AP) *...But isn't that what started this in the first place?*

No Longer Fits on a Postcard
Burma Gives 21 Longer Sentences for Message to UN
Reuter headline

Have it Your Way: Burger King's corporate headquarters has ordered one of its Maryland chain stores to stop issuing coupons for a nearby sporting goods store: "Good for one free box of ammo with gun purchase or 10 percent off." Local police were indignant: "Somebody at Burger King must have lost their mind," the president of the Baltimore police union said. But the management of the Baltimore store was unapologetic. "I'm just someone who sells burgers, not someone who tells you what kind of message we send," manager Michael Sharifi explained. (AP) *...Indeed: most people clearly understand the message you're sending.*

My Turn to Lead: Britain's Royal Air Force has ordered officer cadets to take dancing lessons and etiquette classes to help improve their social skills. "An RAF officer must be able to carry him or herself at all times and not be embarrassed socially," an RAF spokesman said. Officers have traditionally been the cream of the social crop, but high-ranking officers ordered the classes when they discovered new recruits had poor conversational skills and couldn't dance the foxtrot or waltz. (Reuter) ...*Foxtrot, foxhole — whatever.*

Please, After You: The Bozell Worldwide-U.S. News & World Report Quality Quotient poll indicates that Americans think incivility is a serious problem, and it's not only getting worse, but is one of the reasons for the increase in violence. Rude driving habits, language, and children top the list of irritants, but most agree that lawyers, journalists and cops are, for the most part, quite civil. The poll respondents trace the rise in rudeness to political campaigns, television, rock music and talk radio. (AP) ...*And pollsters, who always call at dinnertime.*

Ready, Aim, Lawsuit: Randy Thompson, an employee at the California Bear Credit Union in Los Angeles, is suing his employer for sexual discrimination. "Charles thinks you are peeing on the toilet seat and floor," his supervisor told him. Thompson denies the charge, and has filed a suit alleging that he was made a scapegoat: "No woman was accused" of messing up the unisex restroom, the suit claims. "They believed only a male could be capable." (L.A. Daily Journal) ...*Understandable: most women aren't as well trained for it.*

Anti-Semantic: British rocker Sting is angry at an unauthorized biographer's claim that he had sex with three women at once and that he was a drug addict. "Not everyone who has taken drugs is an addict," he said. And the sex thing? "Of course, I've been in bed with several women at once, I'm a rock star after all," he explained. "But to say I had sex with them simultaneously is pretty dumb." (UPI) ...*That's not a denial, that's bragging.*

Her Special Day: Francis Cardenas was arrested in the murder of his cousin 15 years ago, but he jumped bail and fled to the Philippines. The Glendale, Calif., police never forget a murder. "It appeared he'd left for good," said Detective Sgt. Joe Perkins, who took over the case three years ago when the original detectives retired, but he heard that Cardenas' daughter was getting married somewhere on the west coast. Inspired, detective Art

Frank started calling department stores and asking for the bridal registry, and found her registered at Nordstrom's for a Seattle wedding. Glendale detectives went to Seattle and crashed the rehearsal: sure enough, the suspect was there. "The FBI agents went in and asked him to step outside," Frank said. Cardenas was jailed in Seattle pending extradition to California. (AP) ... *"A gloomy guest fits not a wedding feast."* —*Tell, in "William Tell".*

What's in a Name? A district court in southern Sweden has fined a family $680 for not giving their son a valid first name. The unidentified parents claim the name they chose for the boy is "a pregnant, expressionistic development that we see as an artistic creation." But the court rejects the argument that "Brfxxc- cxxmnpcccclllmmnprxvclmnckssqlbb11116" — pronounced "Albin" — is a real name. The parents plan to appeal. (Reuter) *...It's also unclear whether "Brfxxccxxmnpcccclllm- mnprxvclmnckssqlbb11116" is Swedish, or if that's an English translation.*

Flush With Pride: "We need economic growth," Singapore's Prime Minister Goh Chok Tong says. "We also need to have the resources to support the arts and campaigns to bring about a more gracious lifestyle." How to accomplish this? The Ministry of Environment will conduct a survey on public toilets every four or five years. Goh says the state of public restrooms reflects attitudes over public property and the consideration Singaporeans show each other. Since 1989, Singaporeans have faced fines up to $107 for the first offense of not flushing a public toilet, and up to $714 for third and subsequent offenses. (AP) *...It sounds silly, but once you think about it for a while....*

OK, Best Two out of Three?
Carp Outsmarts Biologist
AP headline

Bleu Funk: The French take three to four times as many tranquil- izers, antidepressants and sedatives than residents of any other

European country, or even the U.S., a French Health Ministry study says. The only drug taken more than antidepressants in France is aspirin. "If the situation doesn't change," warns the study's author, Dr. Edouard Zarifian, "in the near future we'll see an explosion in the medicalization of our existence." (AP) *...Won't telling them this just make them more depressed?*

Threw a Blank Book at Him: Orian Swoveland, 22, in court for sentencing in an auto theft case, wasn't happy with the order of $9,000 in restitution, 60 days in jail and five years' probation — Maui (Hawaii) Circuit Court Judge Boyd Mossman heard Swoveland cursing over it. So Mossman added another item to the sentence: Swoveland must write "I will not swear at the court" 10,000 times. (AP) *...But your honor, I was ordered to swear, so help me God!*

Bad Hair Days: A woman rappelling down a cliff near Sydney, Australia, found herself hanging by her hair when it got caught in her climbing harness. A fellow climber called for help on a portable phone; a policeman rappelled down next to her and cut her free. "I don't know if they were hairdresser's scissors or if it was a real neat job, but they worked," a police spokesman said. Meanwhile, Richard Clunn, 51, is being sued by Michele Rosati for $19,000. Clunn, after arguing with his brother over the cutting ability of a chef's knife, proved its sharpness by cutting off Rosati's two-foot pony tail in a Falls Township, Pa., restaurant. Clunn has already been fined $300 in the case for "harassment". (Reuter, UPI) *...He's lucky: the penalty for impersonating a hairdresser is much more severe.*

You Might be a Terrorist If: "You can easily identify a suspected terrorist," says Epifanio Lambino Jr., chief of the Philippines' Immigration Bureau's Civil Security Unit. "Order him to remove his shoes," he instructs. "Does he have athlete's foot? If so, you may have someone who has undergone rigid military training." Other telltale signs, he says, include a scarred chest and callused hands and elbows from crawling on the ground, and "eyes darting from place to place." Philippine immigration inspectors denied entry to as many as 200 suspected terrorists last year based on such criteria, Lambino said. (AP) ...*It must work. There's no evidence that Ted Kaczynski was able to get by them.*

Billbored: The Florida House of Representatives approved legislation to ban billboards with "sexually suggestive images" along highways in the state. "It's very hard to explain these things, especially to the children of our tourists," said Rep. Bob Starkes, as if he's had to. But Rep. Jeff Stabins says banning the sexy signs is a bad idea. "I believe if you take some of these down it could be a safety hazard because [the signs] keep people awake when they're traveling on the interstates." (UPI) ...*Florida's new safety motto: Drive 55-DD, Stay Alive.*

Consume Mass Quantities: When Randy Watson of Parkville, Md., had a telephone line installed for his computer, he didn't want it listed in his own name. Watson chose "Beldar and Prymaat Conehead" for the directory listing — he uses the name "Beldar" when online. The Coneheads, popular characters from a "Saturday Night Live" show skit about pointy-headed space aliens, excused their weird behavior by claiming "We are from France." A Bell Atlantic spokeswoman says the company plans to "negotiate" with Watson for a correction to the phone book, explaining that "for the book to be of value to our customers, the listings have to be legitimate." (AP) ...*Beldar will be very upset to discover that Ma Bell thinks Prymaat is illegitimate.*

To Protect and to Self-Serve: Burglars twice broke in at Naomi's Busy Mart in Buffalo, N.Y., late on a Saturday night. A video tape from the store's surveillance camera shows the burglars taking cigarettes and lottery tickets. The tapes show something else, too: police officers who responded to the burglar alarms helping themselves to chips, candy bars and soda from the store's shelves. "You see three of them laughing and feasting and drinking," a Busy Mart spokesman said. The three officers have been suspended. (AP) ...*Well, we left payment on the counter, and the burglars must have taken it on their second round. Yeah: that's our story, and we're sticking to it.*

Protect and Serve II: One of the Riverside County, Calif., sheriff deputies involved in the clubbing of two illegal immigrants has sued the county for violating his civil rights in the case. Deputy Tracy Watson claims he was locked in a room by his lieutenant and denied access to an attorney until he completed an incident report about the beating, which was videotaped by a news helicopter. Watson says the lieutenant's actions were intended to get him to incriminate himself. (AP) *...And what, since no one read you your rights you didn't know what they were?*

Customer Service: When a passenger didn't get back to the plane in time for departure after a stopover in Phoenix, an America West Airlines pilot decided the man's luggage shouldn't make the trip either. The pilot stopped the plane, which had already left the gate, and threw the man's bag overboard because he thought it was a "security risk". The FAA is not investigating the case: it's only against the rules to throw baggage overboard if the plane is in the air. (AP) *...If it's a security risk — meaning a bomb may be involved — isn't it a bad idea to throw it onto the pavement from several feet up?*

Danger — Flammable

Warnings Required On Charcoal

AP headline

Jackie Oh My! Auctioneer Sotheby's expected the sale of items from Jacqueline Kennedy Onassis' estate would fetch maybe $4.6 million, tops. But bidding quickly sent prices skyrocketing: a $3,000 rocking chair sold for $453,500; JFK's golf clubs fetched $772,500; JFK junior's high chair and Caroline's rocking horse each brought $85,000; and JFK's humidor sold for $574,500. The sale grossed $34.5 million. (AP) *...Americans are willing to buy anything "Kennedy" except for Ted's explanation of what happened to Mary Jo Kopechne in Poucha Pond.*

Fig Leaves: The Atlanta Committee for the Olympic Games asked Los Angeles Coliseum officials to cover up two nude statues of Olympic athletes for the start of the Olympic torch relay because television viewers might glimpse the statues and find them "indecent". The Atlanta Committee changed its mind after an outcry — and a firm refusal from the Coliseum. The 25-foot statues were modeled after male and female Olympians in the 1984 L.A. games, and have stood at the Coliseum since. "The Greek athletes started out nude in the Olympics," noted Robert Graham, who sculpted the figures. "It's nothing I invented." (L.A. Times) *...Viewers looking for human physical perfection are hardly likely to be offended if they are lucky enough to see it.*

Fighting Words: The California State Assembly has passed another resolution asking the federal government to pay it back for its Civil War costs — "reimbursement of Civil War bonds imposed on the state," said Assemblyman Mickey Conroy. California has been trying since 1861 to collect the debt — now $81.7 million, including interest. The state's claim is based on legislation Congress passed in 1861 to reimburse states who helped in the war. Since then, the U.S. Senate has voted eight times to reimburse California, but the House has never approved the Senate measures. (AP) *...You say the federal government won't honor their written promises? American Indians welcome you to their club.*

World Tour: President Bill Clinton took a man's luggage sightseeing. When leaving a St. Petersburg hotel Clinton stayed in, the President's staff gathered up a pile of luggage from the lobby and sent it all to Moscow. But the pile didn't all belong to Clinton's entourage; part belonged to an Irish businessman, identified only as "Kevin from Donegal". When the mistake was discovered, Clinton returned the man's luggage with a note: "Sorry if we inconvenienced you. Your bags had a great tour of Moscow." (Reuter) *...The best part, though, is the snapshot of his suitcase meeting Gorby.*

Restaurant Critic: New York Attorney Aaron Lichtman doesn't like the chicken restaurant in his building — their sign obscures the sign for his legal practice, and they won't do anything about it, and constant odors from their cooking bother him. So he put up another, hand-lettered, sign in his window right above the restaurant: "BAD FOOD". Kenny Rogers Roasters wasn't amused, and sued Lichtman for $2 million, claiming the sign was a "malicious falsehood". But the state Supreme Court has thrown the suit out, saying the lawyer has a First Amendment right to make his opinion known. Maybe, notes Justice Charles Ramos, the restaurant would have a better case if Lichtman were to stand outside the restaurant and "scream at customers that they would suffer from abdominal distention after eating Roasters' food." (AP) ...*Huh: sounds like the judge has eaten there.*

Lucky in Love: Huang Pin-jen, 27, and Chang Shu-mei, 26, want to end it all. The Taiwanese couple's parents don't approve of their relationship, so they tried to kill themselves by driving over a cliff. When they survived, they tried to hang themselves. That didn't work either, so they held hands and jumped from the 12th-story window of a Taipei hotel. When rescued from the fifth-story roof of the restaurant next door, the couple had no comment. (Reuter, AP) ...*Just go in and order the chicken.*

Canadian Bakin': A Toronto man was startled to be awakened at 4:00 am by police, fire, and ambulance personnel who had responded to an emergency call — the caller had found the man naked inside a coin-operated clothes dryer in a coin-op laundry, and thought he was dead. The man explained he was washing the clothes he was wearing but got cold, so he climbed into the dryer and then fell asleep. (AP) ...*Birthday suits should only be done by hand.*

State of Mind: Spaniard Alberto Porta has declared himself a country. Porta, who now goes by the name Zush, says he got the idea from a schizophrenic he met in a mental hospital in 1968. "Evrugo Mental State" consists of one inhabitant — himself — and he has issued himself a passport so he can move around. Zush has grudgingly adopted a state flag. "I don't need flags and hymns," he says, "but the only way people accept that you have your own state is by using symbols of state. It's purely for diplomatic reasons." (Reuter) ...*The only way to expand his population is to develop a multiple personality — which somehow seems likely.*

Call of Nature: Nearly a quarter of all public telephones in Sabah, on Borneo Island, have been stolen, but Telekom Malaysia officials couldn't figure out why. "Even our telephone manufacturer in Italy was baffled by the thefts," a Telekom spokesman said. An investigation has now revealed why: local fishermen have discovered that when connected to batteries and lowered into the water, the telephone handsets emit a sound which attract fish to their nets. (AP) ...*They don't find out until too late that it's not for them.*

Turned Off the TV
Precautions Taken Against Video Vomit
Reuter headline

Blue Suede Robes: Lehigh University has sponsored a week-long coming out for a new religion, the First Presleyterian Church of Elvis the Divine, where followers "worship" Elvis Presley. They also "should" eat six meals a day (with frequent in-between-meal snacks), pray daily toward Las Vegas, make pilgrimages to the Presley estate Graceland, and boo the "anti-Elvis" — Michael Jackson. Outrageous? "There is a serious side to this," insists Lehigh religion professor Norman Girardot. "All religions start out as small, wacky and cult-like. Some survive. Others do not." Lehigh is located in Bethlehem, Pa. (AP) ...*Yeah, right. Next, I suppose there will be a religion based on science fiction novels.*

Good Benefits: Retired New York and New Jersey employees of the Federated Department Stores received a brochure telling them of their benefits, and listed a telephone number to call for more information. But due to a typo, the number printed was actually for a telephone sex service. The retirees who called the number didn't seem too upset: Federated only got three calls about the typo, and "all of them were laughing about it," a spokeswoman said. (Reuter) ...*How come these typos always turn out to be phone sex lines, and never dial-a-prayer?*

Are We There Yet? Angel Rivera, 33, of Topeka, Kan., allegedly stabbed his girlfriend to death in the front seat of his car, then drove from Topeka to New York City with her body still in the front seat. Relatives convinced him to turn himself in. "He drove to the precinct, he said what he did, then he showed them the body in the car," said a New York Police detective. "She was in the car for two days, dead." Rivera has been charged with second-degree murder and criminal possession of a weapon. (UPI) ...*Police are also retracing his route to see if they can add charges of illegal driving in a car pool lane.*

Paging Dr. Malibu Barbie: First England was hit with mad cow disease. Now comes the terrible toll of "sad doll disease". Doll collectors are lamenting the deterioration of older plastic dolls which cry chemical tears that stain their faces and melt their little heads. "We could see that their heads were becoming misshapen, and brown tears were trickling out of their eyeballs," said Bradford University scientist Howell Edwards, who studied the problem. Worse, an infected doll can actually pass the problem to other nearby dolls. "If just one doll has it, it can affect a whole cabinet," Edwards confirms. The problem: low-quality iron posts which attach the doll's eyeballs to its plastic head. An interaction between the metal and plastic releases acetic acid; the acidic vapor spreads the problem to the other dolls. Washing — and careful drying to prevent the posts from rusting — cures the problem. (Reuter) ...*This is a coverup! We know the disease is actually caused by chopping up old sheep dolls, then using them to mold new human dolls.*

E-I-E-I-O: Rachel Nickle lives right down the street from her ex-husband, Robert Barzyk, and she has to walk right by his house to get to her bus stop. For nine years, she told a Harrisburg, Pa., judge, when she walks by Barzyk's house he made "pig and elephant noises" at her. In September, Nickle says, he added a soundtrack: a cassette recording of "Old MacDonald Had a Farm". The judge agreed that Barzyk was harassing Nickle and sentenced him to 30 days in jail, but Barzyk is out on bond pending an appeal. His attorney says Barzyk was simply playing the children's song for his two daughters. (AP) ...*An injunction*

here, a legal brief there, here a lawyer, there a lawyer, every-
where a lawyer, lawyer.

E-I-E-I-O II: Jacek Soska, Poland's deputy farm minister, has
been named "Peasant of the Year" in a contest after singing a folk
song, arm wrestling, and milking a cow (one-fifth of a pint in 25
seconds). (Reuter) ...*American politicians don't know how much*
milk costs, let alone where it comes from.

Smoke Screen: Most applauded when Boulder, Colo., passed an
ordinance banning smoking in all public buildings. But the Boulder Dinner Theater has challenged the ban — not for the audience,
but for the players. The play "Grand Hotel" has a scene where the
characters smoke, and changing the play without approval would
be a copyright violation. City officials are not impressed: they've
ordered theater owner Ross Haley to comply with the ban or face
90 days in jail and a $1,000 fine. A city "environmental enforce-
ment officer" suggested the theater try a "tobacco-free" cigarette
which emits "non-toxic" smoke. Haley said they tried that, but it
smelled like marijuana. "We actually had the Boulder Police
Department out here because one of the patrons in the show got
up and called the police. They were ready to raid us." (AP)
...*Unfair: giving patrons the "munchies" is just an underhanded*
way to sell more food.

Pop Goes the Weasel: Reverend Stephen Grey, of St. Michael's
Church in Bamford, northern England, was giving communion
when a ferret ran up his cassock. The animal, believed to be a pet,
was ejected from the church after Grey got it out of his clothing.
"I was trained to carry on regardless, but I must admit the prayers
speeded up a bit towards the end," Grey said. (Reuter) ...*That'll*
teach you to demand that He "show you a sign".

Record Highs

Heroin Rains From
Hong Kong Skies

Reuter headline

Yeah, Like That: Matthew Simmons, 21, was found guilty in a London court of using threatening words and behavior at a soccer match. As the prosecutor was asking the court to ban Simmons from future games, Simmons attacked him, shouting "I am innocent! I promise! I swear on the Bible!" It took six policemen and two jailers to overpower Simmons and drag him away from the shaken prosecutor. The court, convinced, added a ban on Simmons from attending any soccer match in England or Wales for a year to his $750 fine — and a week in jail for the in-court assault. (AP) ...*The right to remain silent: it's not just the law, it's a damn good idea.*

Hello? Brig. Gen. Ismael Trujillo Polanco, head of Colombia's Judicial and Investigative Police force, has discovered that drug traffickers cracked into his mobile phone account and ran up a $200,000 phone bill. Investigators have determined the calls were made to coordinate drug shipments to 25 countries. (Reuter) ...*Worse, no one had the courage to trace the calls made on the general's line.*

A Deal's a Deal: Canada's deputy prime minister Sheila Copps has resigned from government because she was unable to fulfill a campaign promise to repeal the national goods and services tax. She briefly resisted, saying her promise to resign if she couldn't defeat the sales tax was a "fast-lip comment" made in the heat of campaigning, but noted "I felt in my heart that I had to resign." (AP) ...*Sheila, please come to the U.S. and give integrity classes to our politicians.*

Hooked: A commercial pilot who drives his helicopter from job to job on the back of a truck knew he was in trouble as soon as he tried to take off: the truck started to rise too. "I just forgot" to remove one of the chains holding the aircraft down, pilot George Hook said. "I got distracted." The chopper was destroyed in the resulting crash and the truck's cab torn apart by the rotor blades, but Hook was unhurt. It was the pilot's second helicopter mishap — he hit a power line in 1977. "I landed upside down and helicopters aren't supposed to land upside down," he said with a laugh. (AP) ...*Hindsight is always 20:20.*

Thou Shalt Not: Linda Siefer, the former church secretary at St. Michael's Roman Catholic Church in Kalida, Ohio, has been convicted of stealing more than $411,000 in cash from church collection plates over a four-year period. The theft was discovered when bank employees wondered why there were never any $20 bills in the church's deposits — prosecutor Dan Gerschutz said Siefer only took the $20 bills, and she took all of them. "If she hadn't gotten greedy, we might not have caught her," he said. "Had she taken a third of the 20s or every third one, she would never have been discovered." (AP) ...*Or, alternatively, 33 percent of them.*

War is Hell: The civil war in Liberia is nothing if not interesting. First, there's the Krahn unit called the "Butt-Naked Brigade" — the unit's soldiers fight naked. That way, "there's nothing between me and God. Only God can protect me," said the Brigade's leader, who calls himself General Butt-Naked. Soldiers of the National Patriotic Front of Liberia, in contrast, wear all the items of clothing they can capture — which isn't much when they fight the Butt-Nakeds. The NPFL advances aggressively until they run out of ammunition and call for more. The Krahn have learned when the NPFL yell "Ammo!" that it's safe to fight back. When a brief truce was called, one soldier explained the calm this way: "He's my brother. You can't kill all the fish in the ocean because then all you have is a great big ocean and no fish." (Reuter) ... *"You can no more win a war than you can win an earthquake."* —Jeannette Rankin, U.S. legislator (1880-1973).

Look it Up: When a White House reporter asked Bill Clinton's press secretary what he thought of a speech by his Republican opponent Bob Dole, Mike McCurry said "That was a lot of kerfuffle." Huh? asked the reporters. "It's a State Department word, K-E-R-F-U-F-F-L-E," McCurry explained without defining the word, which reporters didn't find in their dictionaries. Dole's press secretary offered to help by offering his own definition: "A complimentary term describing advocacy of foreign policy based on American leadership, strength and consistency — as opposed to the weak global leadership, vacillation and inconsistency characterizing the foreign policy of the current

American president," Clarkson Hine said. (AP) *...I thought the citizens were supposed to define the issues in an election. T-H-E E-C-O-N-O-M-Y.*

On the Other Hand: A Canadian man has sued the U.S. Immigration and Naturalization Service for barring his entry into the U.S. based on his convictions for "moral" crimes in 1986. "He was inebriated, he was on a Montreal street, and a nice-looking young woman walked by. He put his hand on her posterior," explains Paul Toutounjian's lawyer, Robert Kolken. U.S. law allows the INS to deny entry of any person who has two convictions for crimes relating to "moral turpitude". But Toutounjian, who pleaded guilty in 1986 to both sexual assault and the commission of an indecent act, argues that since both convictions stemmed from the single incident, he should not be barred from the U.S. based on the "two convictions" rule. "A simple pinch on the fanny does not render him inherently depraved," his lawyer added. (AP) *...Doesn't the use of his entire hand make that more of a complex pinch, Mr. Kolken?*

New Headline Writer Broken in at the Associated Press This Week

Presidential Race Continues

• • •

Library Of Congress Growing

• • •

Clinton Tries To Beat GOP

• • •

Study Links Lung Disease, Air

AP headlines

Paper, Plastic, or Gauze? Antoinette McCullough, 23, a courtesy clerk at a Safeway supermarket in San Francisco, has been charged with two counts of assault with a deadly weapon after two customers accidentally knocked a bottle of beer to the floor. She told the customers to clean it up — she apparently didn't want to since her shift was ending. When they refused, she grabbed a piece of the broken bottle and "things deteriorated from that point," a police spokesman said. "The patrons ended up being stabbed in the face by the clerk with pieces of the bottle." The shoppers were treated at a nearby hospital. A Safeway spokeswoman tried to put the attack in perspective: "This is not typical of our stores," she said. (AP) *...Don't apologize: it's the first time a Safeway clerk has offered customers some service.*

Look What the Cat Dragged In: Kenji Fukai's cat brings home the bacon. In addition to a recent dead bird, Fukai noticed the cat also brought a plastic bag with 160,000 yen (about US$1500) in cash into his Tokyo house. Meanwhile, Maurice, a Wellington, New Zealand, feline, has been nicking knickers — so far, about 60 undershirts and bras taken in nocturnal raids around the neighborhood. "Obviously my stuff wasn't good enough," said the cat's female owner, who was not identified. A vet suggested a dose of hormones might calm him down, but his owner isn't convinced. "Maurice is the calmest cat in the world. If he was any calmer he would be dead." (AP, Reuter) *...Hormones could be a bad idea: he's already cross-dressing as it is.*

Bite Me: When Valentin Grimaldo was bitten by a poisonous coral snake, he kept his head. The snake didn't fare as well. Grimaldo, walking near Encino, Texas, was bitten on the hand. He grabbed the snake and bit its head off, then "he skinned it and used the skin as a tourniquet to keep the venom from spreading," said a hospital spokeswoman. Grimaldo survived. His brother is keeping the head as a souvenir. (AP) *...Macho Grimaldo, coming up on the next Geraldo!*

Spring in the Air: Residents in Stigtomta, southern Sweden, have staged "Pee Outdoors Day" to call attention to the problem with a nearby lake. A local environmental group, Save the Hallbo Lake, says that the local sewage treatment plant is killing the lake's fish and plants by pumping too much nitrogen into the water. Even the village priest took part in the event, as did 2000 other residents. (Reuter) *...Plus, the lake is now significantly larger.*

That Last Coat of Paint was a Mistake: The California Highway Patrol took a tape measure to Sheik Hamad Bin Hamdan Al-Nahayan's car and determined his limousine isn't street-legal. The Lincoln limo, which has five axles and is articulated in the middle to get around corners, is 66.5 feet long — 18 inches longer than state law allows. But Ultra Custom Coach, which built the 7-ton, $1.8 million car, says they're modifying it so the Sheik can go back on the road. "We've taken some of the plastic off the bumpers and we're tightening up the clearance a little bit," said general manager Kraig Kavanagh. (AP) *...Yeah, but now the swimming pool isn't regulation Olympic length anymore.*

Take a Bite Out of Crime: Kendall Coffey, the U.S. Attorney for the Miami, Florida, area, has resigned his position after a topless dancer in an adult entertainment club accused him of biting her while she was giving him a private performance. In a statement, Coffey said he must leave, "because my family has paid too great a price for the sacrifices that accompany public service." Uh, anything to say about the dancer's charges, Kendall? "I have concerns about the possible impact on the important work on my office," he said. (UPI) *...She should get tested: I've heard him described as a rabid prosecutor.*

Hand Over the Money: Thomas W. Passmore, 32, was working on a construction project in Norfolk, Va., when he noticed a mark on his hand. It looked like "666" to him. He remembered his Bible: "If thy right hand offend thee, cut it off." Passmore picked up his circular saw and complied. Taken to a nearby hospital, he refused to give consent to surgery, saying he would go to hell if they reattached his hand. Hospital officials, unsure what to do, consulted a judge, who told the hospital to follow their patient's wishes. Now, Passmore is suing the hospital for $3.35 million, saying they should have overruled his orders and forced him to have the surgery. He said the hospital is liable because he told them he had a history of mental problems, and had not slept much recently. (AP) *...And if they had sewn it back on, he'd be suing* *for $3.35 million for religious persecution. Nice scam.*

Among Other Things
Condoms Held Up by Elections
Reuter headline

Sister Kicked Her Keester: Catholic nuns at St. Anne's convent in Madras, India, are taking karate classes to protect them from local thugs. Their focus and self-discipline make them "much better than any normal strong person, even a commando," said their instructor, Shihan Husaini. And he should know: he has trained commandos. About 50 nuns have completed training so far. "When I went to a school in a village a few months ago, some people threatened me and I fled from there," says Sister Arulmozhi. "Now I feel so bold I am just waiting to go back." Sister Yanmitho agrees: "These days if I am attacked, I cannot turn the other cheek," she said. "I am ready to defend myself, although I will still pray for my attackers." (AP) ...*They'll need it, sister. They'll need it.*

Would You Like Fries with That? Britain's program to destroy much of their stock of cattle in an effort to stamp out "mad cow" disease is not progressing as rapidly as planned. "There is no way we can use conventional incinerators because that capacity isn't available," said Roger Freeman, the agricultural minister responsible for the program. "We need to look at something radical, and we are trialling different incineration methods." Like what? Freeman is checking with electric utilities to see if they can burn cow parts to help generate electricity. Freeman must figure out how to burn 750,000 cattle to ashes in the next year. (Reuter) ...*I've heard of mood lighting, but this is ridiculous.*

Buff and Polish: Glen Jarvis was bored by his job working with computers, so he decided to go out on his own. His new company, "Butler in the Buff", charges $15 an hour for Jarvis to clean houses in Kansas City, Mo., in the nude. Customers may watch, but Jarvis makes it clear that he's only there to clean. Meanwhile, a new business in Portland, Maine, "Rent-A-Husband", is available "for those jobs that never get done." Owner Kaile Warren Jr. says the name "gives handymen an identity. Nobody can remember Jones Construction." And while all the rental husbands so far are male, "I think it would be neat to have female husbands," he says. (Reuter, AP) ...*I see an interesting merger in the future of these companies.*

Not Guilty: Damon Nance, 19, admitted it: "The cross was burned in order to tell black people to stay out of this neighborhood," he told police in Peoria, Ill. He pleaded guilty to a hate crime and was sentenced to three years in prison. But Nance was freed from prison, his conviction nullified, because a judge has ruled that the law only applies when the victim of the crime is in a "protected class" defined in the hate crime law, and Nance's target was white — a 16-year-old girl who was dating a black man. Prosecutors are thinking of filing new charges: criminal damage to property, a much lesser crime. (AP) ...*Exactly what happens when you have a society based on law, but forgets about justice.*

Sugar Water: The fight between Coke and Pepsi has reached orbit. On the U.S. space shuttle *Endeavour,* astronauts worked to fix their Coke dispenser — provided by the cola giant — which was putting out foam instead of the icy soft drink. Almost simultaneously, Pepsi said they had begun filming a commercial at the Russian *Mir* space station, a privilege the company said cost them "a seven-figure sum". In the commercial, space-walking cosmonauts film the "deployment" of a replica Pepsi can into orbit. (AP, Reuter) ...*My kind of cold war.*

I Say! "Britain is becoming ruder," says Dr. Digby Anderson after a study of manners in the country. "Loutishness on the streets, slovenly and aggressive dress, swearing, cheating sportsmen, parents aping the style and slang of teenagers and a false chumminess from doctors and other professions point to a crisis in manners." But meanwhile, Germans are becoming much more polite, academics there say. "There are certain periods in history when the question of etiquette becomes topical again," says Inga Wolff, editor of "Style and Etiquette" magazine, and in Germany, now is one of those times. Why? "Because the European Union has grown so close together and leaders' visits have become so frequent, nowadays they are more like a visit to a neighbor's house." (Reuter, 2) ... *"No one can be as calculatedly rude as the British, which amazes Americans, who do not understand studied insult and can only offer abuse as a substitute."* —*Paul Gallico, U.S. novelist (1897-1976).*

Let Me Make This Clear: Mobile phone giant Nokia is angry that their new simplified handset has been dubbed a "bimbophone" by industry pundits. Spokesman Lars Bjarnemark says the phone isn't designed just for dumb blondes: "That's not what we're saying. They're not interested in the extra features so why sell them," he asked. Then who is the new "rinGo" designed for? It is "aimed at women, young families, students and pensioners," he said. "Our market research shows that there are quite a number groups that have refrained from buying a phone because [the] digital technology is too complicated for them." (Reuter) ...*Ah: they're not bimbos, but idiots. Thanks for the clarification.*

Right where it Hurts
Colombia Smacks U.S. in Rhetoric
AP headline

Madvertising: With the "mad cow" scare in full force, the Europe-wide ban on British cows has left many farmers strapped for cash and wondering what to do with their herds. Harry Goode says his idea to make ends meet "is a bit of a gimmick, but an interesting one." He's selling advertising space on the side of his cows, which graze near Birmingham. Passing motorists are the audience; Goode has already sold eight ads, charging 300 pounds (US$450) per week for the cow placards. "They are losing money while they are feeding so they might as well start paying for their upkeep," Goode said. (Reuter) ...*Wonder if he's tried "For Sale"?*

It's an Ad, Ad World II: Cistercian monks living on Caldey, a small island off Wales, have broken their vow of silence — in television commercials. The brothers fund their abbey with cash brought in by tourists, but a recent oil spill has killed off the tourist trade. They tried to sell some of their prize cattle, but couldn't because of the mad cow ban. So it's on to TV with ads trying to lure the tourists back. "We have a strict rule of silence," Brother Robert says, "but we also have to live in the modern world." (Reuter) ... *Why?*

Go Ahead, Make My Day: The governor of Ohio has been fined $1,500 by the Federal Aviation Administration for ordering his pilot to take off despite a flight ban in effect because President Clinton was visiting nearby. Gov. George Voinovich himself spoke to the control tower over the plane's radio, and was told the Secret Service's "no-fly order" would be in effect until the president left. "I'm going to tell them to go screw themselves, OK," the governor told the tower. "If they don't like it, fine. They can shoot us down." (AP) ... *Considering Voinovich is a possible vice presidential candidate under Dole, Clinton may try to exercise that shoot-down option later.*

Stamped Them Out: Hong Kong has decided to stop issuing stamps featuring Queen Elizabeth II. "We ... need a stamp which will take us through a period where we're under British sovereignty into a period when we are under Chinese sovereignty," said the island's postmaster general. Britain's queen has been on Hong Kong's stamps for 134 years. (Reuter) ... *If you can't join 'em, don't lick 'em.*

Tux Measurements, Line A; Fingerprinting, Line B: Some high schools in the Chicago area are running background checks on prom dates. Students who bring dates that don't go to the same school must submit their dates' names, and the school checks their criminal records. "We have to provide a safe environment for the kids," said a teacher on a prom committee. But the mother of one girl whose date was rejected denounced the practice. "We're talking about going to a dance for a few hours," she said. "It's not like he wants a job." (AP) ... *You can take my daughter to a hotel, but you better not try to get a job making her hamburgers. Got it?*

Give Him the Finger: Workers demolishing a house in Sydney, Australia, found two human fingers in the rubble. Police, noting one had a "nicely manicured" nail, started an investigation. But a man who once lived in the house heard news accounts of the find and stepped forward to claim the digits. The eight-fingered man said that he had an accident with a circular saw while living in the house 25 years ago, and didn't realize the fingers had been left there. (Reuter) ...*That's just like a guy to not know where his fingers have been.*

Crumpet Strumpet: U.S. astronaut Shannon Lucid, half-way through her tour on board the Russian *Mir* space station, is enjoying her stay, she says. And the cosmonauts on board like having her there. "She is waiting for us and when we come back [from space walks] she helps us out and makes hot tea," says cosmonaut Yuri Onufrienko. Anything else, Yuri? Yes! "In addition to tea, she also does excellent work in maintaining systems and organizing things aboard the ship." Before she launched into space, a Russian space official noted it would be a good idea to have a woman on board, "because women love to clean." (AP) ...*Those Russians are so boorish. Tea service is more properly the butler's job.*

Marion Barry Wannabe: The mayor of Copperhill, Tenn., has had her marijuana plants confiscated. Janelle Kimsey, who is serving her second term as mayor, had several potted pot plants on her porch, police said. Officers got a search warrant and searched her home, but no other drugs were found. The mayor said she planned to turn the pot in to police after it was fully grown, but the police chief said he hadn't heard of the plan. Why did she do it? "We made a drug bust a couple of months ago and the citizens said they wanted to know what it [marijuana] looked like," she said. "Dumb me, I didn't know I couldn't do it." (AP) ...*Sounds like a slogan for her reelection campaign.*

After What Happened to Rabin, I'm Not
Sure Bibi Will Appreciate This
Clinton: Give Netanyahu a Shot
AP headline

Don't Call Us, We'll Call You: Police in Philadelphia got reports that Jeremiah Allen, 29, had kidnaped his ex-girlfriend and was holding her hostage at his apartment. Officers got an idea. "Police called him, told him to bring the woman down to the station, and he said, 'OK'," a police spokesman said. He not only brought the woman to the station, he brought the gun he used in the abduction. Allen was arrested and charged with kidnaping, aggravated assault and weapon offenses. (AP) ...*Imagine the success they could have with completely random calls....*

Only in Los Angeles: Kody "Monster" Scott, paroled from a California prison after serving four years for armed robbery, allegedly punched out his parole officer and went on the lam. But the prison author of "Monster: The Autobiography of an L.A. Gang Member," which brought a $200,000 advance from the Atlantic Monthly Press, still found time to keep in daily touch with his agent and sit for a front-page interview in the L.A. Times. He got his nickname from a detective who saw the kicked-in face of one of Scott's victims; "only a monster" could have done that, the detective said. Los Angeles police finally caught up with Scott and took him into custody. They found him in front of a house, signing autographs for fans. A police spokesman noted that Scott "said he wanted to go back to prison and write some more." (AP) ...*Crime doesn't pay, but publishers are making sure writing about it does.*

Loo Queue: Beijing's Museum of the Revolution has opened a new exhibit showcasing advanced Chinese toilet technology. A spokesman for a toilet manufacturer exhibiting its wares noted "people are demanding more and more from their toilets." Meanwhile, a newspaper in Bucharest says there are only 19 functional toilets available in the city for tourists. Most toilets in the city, they warned, are just "too gruesome" to use. However, the Romanian daily Evenimentul Zilei notes, "the toilets run by the cemetery administration work, are clean, and there is no charge." (Reuter, 2) ...*People are just dying to get in there.*

Loopholes: The IRS has flunked its audit. A General Accounting Office probe of the Internal Revenue Service found that "fundamental persistent problems remain uncorrected" at the tax-collecting agency for the fourth straight year. The IRS's books don't balance, the GAO says, it can't account for much of its spending, and it can't show reliable numbers for the amount of overdue taxes the government is owed. "Nobody in the private sector would take that long to identify who owes them money," a GAO director said. The IRS's new chief financial officer insists tax money has not "somehow been misappropriated," but the agency "still [has] much to do" to improve. (AP) ...*I'm sure you'll accept that as an excuse from taxpayers you audit, yes?*

You're in a Heap of Trouble, Boy: Calling it "a clear violation" of South Carolina's decency law, Lance Cpl. Kevin Cusack let Patti Redden off with a warning. A sticker in her car's back window, which featured a drawing of Calvin of "Calvin and Hobbes" comic fame urinating on the letters "IRS", was the offending infringement, the highway patrolman said. Chilled by the threat of arrest, "I went ahead and took it off then because I didn't want to get stopped again," Redden told reporters. The drawing's First Amendment charm was lost on lawyers from the Universal Press Syndicate, which distributes the comic. "We say more power to the South Carolina Highway Patrol," attorney Tom Gill said. (AP) ...*The IRS must love it; who needs 'jack-booted thugs' when you have media attorneys denouncing political parody?*

Let Them Eat Cake: Clarkstown, N.Y., has two problems: hungry homeless people, and a huge flock of geese whose droppings contaminate local waterways and park lands. "One goose produces one pound of droppings a day," said Rockland County Health Commissioner Marvin Thalenberg. "With 350 geese, you do the arithmetic." What to do? Town officials plan to round up

350 geese for processing in a local poultry plant, and the meat will be given to a local charity for the homeless. (AP) ...*Town officials deny that the project is officially called "Operation Soylent Green".*

Sign Here: Jeffrey J. Pyrcioch and Heather M. Green, both 19, thought they had figured out the perfect crime, police in West Lafayette, Ind., said: they wrote checks using disappearing ink. Checks totaling $2,000 were passed around town, but when merchants looked at them later they were blank. How did police track the pair down? Pyrcioch's name was printed on the checks by the bank — in permanent ink. The two face eight years in prison on fraud and theft charges. (AP) ...*If you listen carefully at John Scopes' grave, you can hear him screaming, "I was right!"*

That's Nothing — the Republicans Plan
a Nice Assortment of Cognacs
Democrats Tap Miller
For Convention
AP headline

Bedrock: Crews excavating a lot in Los Angeles for the new headquarters of the Metropolitan Water District have uncovered a 19th-century "red light district." Dr. Adrian Praetzellis, an archeologist who directed the dig, said the four-acre area supported "sex on an industrial scale." Trash is of special interest: "People don't edit their garbage," he said, noting a bottle of "Darby's Prophylactic Fluid" and other artifacts. "The things they throw out tell us all kinds of stuff about their lives." To help preserve history, some of the cathouse bricks will be used to build the new office building. (AP) ...*Nothing changes in L.A.: it still runs on sex on an industrial scale.*

Joystick: "Virtual Girlfriends" is a hit in Tokyo, too. The video game makes players steer a boy through high school, where he must look nice, get good grades, and — especially — be popular.

"The game is like a dream come true, because you can ask a lot of girls out on dates," says the manufacturer's spokesman. "In the game you can be brave because you can't go wrong." If the player makes the right moves, the virtual schoolgirl will say "I love you." Fans are cheering a promised sequel, where they can profess their love back to the machine. "The fun lies in the process of finding out what makes a girl happy," one player said. (UPI) ...*Here's a thought: ask a real one.*

All Aboard: A bus driver in Orange County, Calif., has been fired for refusing to pass out coupons for free hamburgers to passengers. "I told them that I don't eat dead cows and no one else needs to, either," said Bruce Anderson, a vegetarian. A transit agency spokesman said handing out coupons to riders is part of the job, and if Anderson won't do his $16.60-an-hour job, he has to be "held accountable". Anderson is unrepentant. "What I did probably saved at least half a cow," he said. (AP) ...*For the cow's sake, let's hope it was the first half.*

Animal Rites II: The gopher museum in Torrington, Alberta, Canada, is making its debut despite a year-long campaign by animal rights activists to stop it. In 31 scenes, 54 stuffed gophers, culled from local farm fields, are set up with clothing and tiny props to depict a day in the life of Torrington: they play hockey, get their hair done, shoot pool, fish, and even rob a bank. The locals didn't think much of the attempt by outsiders to keep the museum from opening: Mayor Harold Ehrman told them to "go stuff themselves." But Diane Kurta, head of Torrington's tourism committee, liked the controversy. "They've given us thousands of dollars of free publicity," she said. (AP) ...*Coming soon: a new scene with the gophers tying animal rights activists to the town railroad tracks.*

Charmed, I'm Sure: Russell Crowe said he didn't want to cut grass for a living for the rest of his life. He thought he might make more money selling snake venom, which is used in some medicines. But his plan slipped away when a neighbor found an escaped cobra in her garden and called authorities. A fish and game officer found Crowe's nest of 40 poisonous snakes stacked in boxes in his rented room, and charged him with housing snakes in an unsafe and unsanitary manner. The Brevard County, Fla., man was sentenced to probation, but only if Crowe disposes of the remaining snakes quickly. And, the judge cautioned, "they are not just something you can give away to anybody." (Reuter) *...Maybe he should try opening a museum.*

Mail Call: Jane Stewart just got a letter. The post, which contained a photograph, a newspaper clipping about a cousin's wedding, and other family news, was mailed on March 17, 1972 and bore an 8-cent stamp. Since then, it had been kept with 2,000 other pieces of mail stolen by a former post office clerk, who stored it all at his home. Upon his arrest, the mail was recovered and sent on its way. Stewart was happy to get the letter. "It's still news to me, even though it's 24 years late," she said. (AP) *...Apparently, the Stewart family doesn't talk much.*

Night Light: Merlina Merton, a Phillipine-based expert on the Chinese architectural art of *feng shui,* wants you to have good sex. First, a home's bathroom door should definitely not open toward the honeymoon bed, he said. But even more important is the placement of the television: "Radiation [from the TV set] can disturb the energy field of the bed," Merton said. Further, he advises, when watching adult movies, the TV should be angled toward the bed. (Reuter) *...Huh: I thought the best place for the TV during sex was in another room.*

Hassle Huff: When David Letterman took his talk show to Southern California briefly last year, he asked real Los Angeles County beach lifeguards to recite a "Top 10" list of lifeguard pick-up lines (sample: "Coast Guard regulations, miss, I have to inspect you for sand mites.") Their boss didn't see the show, but heard about it when it was re-run recently. One of the lifeguards from the show has now been suspended, and the others reprimanded, for not asking permission to appear in their official bathing suits or to pose on their lifeguard trucks. Chief lifeguard Don Rohrer said the lifeguards' behavior was "inexcusable" and "set back the reputation of lifeguards 50 years." (AP) *...Is that the same 50 years that "Baywatch" set them back, or a different 50?*

Like Father, Like Son: Wayne Hamilton, 41, of Ridgeville, Ind., has been charged with felony neglect of a dependent after a 3-year-old boy living with him was seen sitting in his underwear, smoking a cigarette and drinking a beer. "Yeah, man. Smokin'," the lad told a county welfare worker. "Cigarettes is cool, man." The boy is said to have drunk as many as three beers at a time. Hamilton faces three years in jail. (AP) *..It's despicable for a parent not to teach a kid better grammar..*

Imelda Has Such Fine Childhood Memories
70,000 Stuffed Animals Recalled
AP headline

Survival of the Witless: When James Lertola, 20, and Brian Witham, 25, escaped from the Marble Valley prison in Rutland, Vt., they had a plan. In writing. "Drive to Maine, get safer place to stay, buy guns, get Marie, get car — Dartmouth, do robbery, go to New York." When a Dartmouth, Mass., police officer approached that car, which was stolen, the two ran, and police found the to-do list. Lertola and Witham were arrested in New York, shortly after the bus from Massachusetts arrived. (AP) *...Go to court, implicate other guy, cop plea, do time.*

Big Ideas: Bryan Naranjo, 18, of Bogota, Colombia, is "delighted" to have been named the smallest man in Latin America. The 27.9 inch-tall man says the distinction "should help me meet more people," especially women. But the women don't have to be short: "I like all kinds of women," he said. "Blondes, with green eyes, tall ones, and especially those who wear miniskirts." (Reuter) *...I'll bet.*

Hardtime Hotel: The state of South Carolina is trying to get control of its own prisons — control taken away by the federal government, not the inmates. Attorney General Charlie Condon said he's looking forward to the end of federal control, instituted in 1985 because of overcrowding and poor conditions, so the state can pack in inmates "like sardines". Condon says inmates "are not being mistreated in South Carolina prisons. If anything, you can make the argument that they enhance their status by being sent to prison." (AP) *...I know a lot of people think that about South Carolina, but I didn't expect a state official to admit it.*

Paging Dr. Kildare: A British doctor confined to a wheelchair for 18 months has finally been able to diagnose his own illness by watching a soap opera on TV. "The handsome hero Dr. Standish has an old flame visiting — a jazz singer who is breathless and tired," said Dr. Rodney Haverson, 52, of London. "As I watched I was ticking off her symptoms and thinking 'Yep, I've got that, and that, and that'." The diagnosis, as provided by "The Flying Doctors" and confirmed by a neurologist: myasthenia gravis. Haverson's doctor has begun treatment. (UPI) *...Or at least he will, as soon as he can consult with the show's writers as to the therapeutic options.*

We Can Make Beautiful Music Together: An inventor in Budapest has unveiled his newest innovation: a musical condom. When unrolled, it begins its serenade. Users so far have a choice of two tunes: "You Sweet Little Dumbbell" or "Arise, Ye Worker". (AP) *...And, coming soon, "God Rest Ye Merry Gentlemen".*

Arise, Ye Worker II: Police in Melbourne, Australia, are looking for burglars who stole drugs from an impotence clinic there. If used incorrectly, the drugs can cause five-day erections, causing "extreme discomfort". Police said they "are looking for someone who is very embarrassed or very tired." (Reuter) *...Or, more likely, women.*

Model Citizen: "If I'm going to draw someone else nude, I want to know what it feels like on the other side of the pencil," said teacher Mark Jesionowski from Central Catholic High School in Toledo, Ohio. In addition to his job teaching art and religion at Central High, Jesionowski has been posing nude for art students at another school. "I honestly did not know there was anything wrong with it. This is the way God put us together," he said. But Rev. Michael Billian, president of Central High, says nudes are OK in the Sistine Chapel, but posing for such art is not OK for a high school teacher. "There are issues revolving around being a role model, of being a Christian model," he said. He forced Jesionowski to resign from his side job, under a "morals" clause in his contract. (AP) ...*Guess what, Mike: Michelangelo didn't paint the Chapel with his eyes closed.*

Best Seller, with a Bullet: The Dutch Voluntary Euthanasia Society, tired of waiting for "the legal availability of the means to end one's life," has decided to publish its own self-help guide to suicide. A spokesman said that because of the lack of medical assistance, "some 1,500 to 1,800 people [in the Netherlands] are forced to seek recourse to methods which place a heavy burden on those around them, like jumping under a train." The information, he said, "is already available — we are merely providing it in accessible form in response to a clear need." (Reuter) ...*Satisfaction guaranteed or your life back.*

Missed Manners: Nebiu Demeke, 23, hijacked a plane in Europe and forced it to the U.S. But, he said, he was nice about it. "I hijacked it politely," he told the court during his trial in New York. "I freely surrendered. I helped the FBI," he said, adding he only hijacked the plane because the U.S. denied him a visa for entry. Unmoved, the judge sentenced him to 20 years. (AP) ...*After which he will be asked — politely — to leave the country.*

You'd Have to Be Stupid to Think That
Britons Say They're Getting Dumber
Reuter headline

Off the Hook: Bob Ringewold knew the rental car agency might not believe how his vehicle was damaged, so he brought along some evidence. Then he took a big breath and told them what happened: he and a friend were driving near Lake Michigan when an eagle flew over with a five-pound fish in its talons. The fish managed to wriggle free — and hit the car smack on the roof, denting it. Agent Rick Ireland of Avis believed every word. "A person couldn't make up a story like that," he said. "That's the oddest story I've ever heard." Ringewold's evidence? The fish — a sucker. (AP) ...*There's one of those born every minute.*

Stressbuster: Concerned with a recent rash of "road rage", which has resulted in a number of violent incidents between drivers, a British politician has proposed roadside entertainment as a possible solution. Jugglers, recommends Conservative John Butcher. And perhaps other performers: "I could weave in and out of the cars, provided they weren't going too fast," a unicyclist suggested, "although I think I would have to drop my fire juggling act because of all the petrol around." (UPI) ...*It's a good idea: rather mimes and jugglers than innocent people.*

At Least It's the Right Direction: Yuba City is celebrating. The northern California farming town has moved off the bottom of "Money" magazine's ranked list of 300 U.S. cities. One notch, from 300 to 299. "That stinks," said one local 12-year-old. "It should be at least 100." But Mayor Pat Hearne took the next-to-bottom ranking in stride. "I look at it as being one of the best 300 places to live," she said. (AP) ...*Don't forget, Pat: that kid will be able to vote in just six years.*

Film at 11:00: When Heather Jaehn returned to her El Cajon, Calif., home with her boyfriend after an outing, she realized she had forgotten her keys and was locked out. While the unnamed man looked for an open window, the 100-pound Jaehn, 25, climbed to the roof and started down the chimney, only to become stuck partway. The boyfriend tried for three hours to rescue her before resorting to calling the fire department. Getting warm in the confined space, Jaehn took off her sweater; when fire fighters finally hauled her up in front of a bevy of news and TV cameras, she was "naked from the waist up," said battalion chief Ed Jarrell. "I think she's taking it better now than she was at first," Jarrell said, adding that "without a doubt, in my 21 years, this has been my most unusual human rescue." (Reuter) ...*Such a cliché: locked out but the top was down the whole time.*

Santa Wannabe II: Felix Rivera wanted a beer, but the San Antonio, Texas, Pik Nik store where he usually shopped was closed for the night. So he found some used cooking oil out back, greased up his body, and slid in through a rooftop air vent. And got stuck, with his legs dangling from the store's ceiling. Luckily, he set off the store's burglar alarm. Fire fighters took an hour to rescue him, by which time Joe Castellano, the store's manager, had arrived. "He walked up to me and said, 'Sorry, man. All I wanted was a beer'," Castellano said. "Because of the alarm, he was pretty deaf after he left." (AP) ...*Careful: when his head clears, he'll want to sue you for that.*

This Ain't Rocket Science: CERN, the European Laboratory for Particle Physics at the border between France and Switzerland, couldn't get their particle accelerator — the largest in the world — to start up. After five days, technicians found the problem: there were two beer bottles in the 27-km collider's vacuum chamber. Empty beer bottles. The investigation as to how they got there continues. (Reuter) ...*This is just a suggestion, but they should probably talk to Felix Rivera.*

Take Me Out to the Ball Game: Promoters of the idea saw it as a way to attract attention to their minor league baseball team: for one game, fans would be allowed to attend in the nude. But the managers of the Palm Springs (Calif.) Suns were overwhelmed with phone calls and had to cancel: they couldn't meet the demand for seats. "After thousands and thousands of phone calls, we just realized the stadium, which holds only 3,500 people, was not big enough to handle it," said Tom Mulhall, who thought up the "Nude Night" promotion. A typical Suns game draws less than 1,000 fans. (Reuter) ...*Buy me some peanuts and Crackerjack; I don't care if I ever get back.*

Show and Tell: Teachers in Saskatchewan complained that the "supplementary demonstrators" they were provided for ninth-grade sex education classes were "inappropriate", so the Canadian province's department of education is trying to sell all 1,000 that they bought. The what? The wooden, erect penis models used to demonstrate condom installation. So far, only 46 have been sold. (Reuter) ...*But it's so important these kids be properly educated to avoid splinters!*

Try Not to Think About It

Worry May Stunt Girls' Growth

AP headline

Extra *True* Headlines . . . .

**Don't Come Back Until You Find a Cat o' Nine Tails
and a Pair of Handcuffs**

4 Punished For Scavenger Hunt

AP

• • •

Saw it When they Bent Over

Bottom Line Spots Crack
in Toilet Roll Market

Reuter

• • •

That's Our Story, and We're Sticking To It

Americans Say TV Makes
Them Smoke Dope

Reuter

• • •

There's Just No Quality in this Country Anymore

No Federal Standard For Deaths

AP

• • •

If Nature Calls, Don't Answer

Tot Ticketed For Going Wee-Wee

AP

Especially if your Forehead Gets in Your Eyes
Study: Fat, Blindness Linked
AP

• • •

Stop the Presses!!
Ex-Lawmaker Found Innocent
AP

• • •

Bordeaux on the Rocks
Eat Like Caveman, Drink Like French — Live Longer
Reuter

• • •

Guns Don't Kill, Extremely Confused Headline Writers Do
Gun Used Couldn't Fire Itself
AP

• • •

Permission Granted
Media May Ignore Foreign News
AP

• • •

Jump Start
Sex Workers Say Penises Don't Work
Reuter

And Then Wrestled to the Ground by the Secret Service
Irish Girl Touches Clintons
AP

• • •

Finally Proven in Clinical Trials
Politicians Full Of Hot Air
Reuter

• • •

Was Bound to Happen
Web Artist's Heads Explode
AP

• • •

He Was Such a ...*Quiet* Man
Killer Had Behavioral Problem
AP

• • •

Too Big to Swallow
Man Chokes Pit Bull
AP

• • •

Not Doing Anything Else That Day Anyway
Spain May Vote For Change
AP

Just Like Mom Used to Make

Girl's Cupcake Causes Fire
AP

...

Friends, Romans, Countrymen

Saddam: No More Ear Amputation
AP

...

Damn Near Impossible

Life Tough After Death Row
AP

...

Not a Good Enough Reason to Bring
Back "The Partridge Family"

"Lonely, Failed" Stars May Hold Secret to Universe
Reuter

...

What Else is New?

Women Sacrifice Comfort for Cleavage
Reuter

...

Mouth Not Connected

Study Finds No Link Between Breastfeeding, Brains
Reuter

Employment Contract Provisions Strictly Upheld

Suicide Bomber Blew Self Up

AP

• • •

Opposition had Little to Lose

Prosecution Loses Playboy Suit

AP

• • •

Go Figure

Arrests Made At Marijuana Fest

AP

• • •

Occupational Hazard

Soap Characters Are
Sick in the Head

UPI

• • •

That Explains a Lot

Music Industry Meets On Drugs

AP

• • •

Win Some, Lose Some

England Fans Too Tired to Riot
After Bitter Defeat

Reuter

And, Last...

Judge Not, Lest Ye Be Judged
Christ Resigns as Police Chief
Indianapolis Star

About the Author . . . .

Randy Cassingham has a university degree in Journalism, but he has never been a conventional news reporter. His unbounding sense of curiosity has led him to explore a number of careers, including commercial photographer, freelance writer, editor, publisher, ambulance paramedic, search and rescue sheriff's deputy, process engineer, business consultant, software designer, and after-dinner speaker.

He is a leading proponent of the Dvorak keyboard, an ergonomic alternative to the common "Qwerty" layout found on most computers and typewriters — except Randy's, where you'll find Dvorak layouts.

Randy is single and lives in Boulder, Colorado with Clancy, "a mixed holstein". (Photograph by Dave Casler.)

Get More *True*

This is True compilations come out every year, pulling together a year's worth of Randy's column plus *extra* stories and headlines that didn't fit into his weekly space. Order the books through your favorite bookstore, or get them directly from us. Either way, be sure to "Get One for Every Bathroom in the House!"

• • •

☐ Send me Volume 1! I need ___ copies of *This is True: Deputy Kills Man With Hammer* at $11.00 each plus $2.00 shipping*.

☐ I need ___ more copies of Volume 2, *This is True, Glow-in-Dark Plants Could Help Farmers* for $11.00 each plus $2.00 shipping*.

* Only one $2.00 shipping charge is required per order, no matter how many copies are ordered. (U.S., Canada, FPO/APO only. Offer may be withdrawn at any time. Write for shipping rates for other countries, or see our web page.)

☐ I'm desperate to get a regular *True* fix every week by e-mail. Please e-mail me information on Internet subscriptions!

☐ *This is True* isn't in any newspapers near me, and it should be. I'm attaching the name, address and phone number of a paper near me that needs to carry *True* every week.

• • •

☐ Check or Money Order Enclosed

☐ Charge my: ☐ Visa ☐ Mastercard ☐ Discover ☐ AmEx

Card # _____-_____-_____-_____ (Expires: ____/____)

Name: _____

Address: _____

City: _____ State/Prov: _____

Zip/Postal Code: _____ Country: _____

E-mail address: _____

Mail this form with check or credit card information to Freelance Communications, PO Box 17326, Boulder CO 80308 USA, or fax with your credit card information to +1-500-442-TRUE, or see our web page: http://www.thisistrue.com/

What is the Dvorak Keyboard?

Randy Cassingham doesn't type on the same keyboard as most people. "As a writer, it makes sense for me to use the Dvorak. It's easier to learn and use, easier on my hands, and more productive," he says. "It is criminal to start kids out on anything else."

Long a proponent of the Dvorak (pronounced "duh-VOR-ack") layout, designed by Dr. August Dvorak (1894-1975) and colleagues at the University of Washington in the 1920s, Randy wrote "the" book about the design and is a technical consultant to the American National Standards Institute keyboard standards committee.

The Dvorak was designed to work in concert with the physical structure of the hand as well as the English language. The common "Qwerty" keyboard was designed in the 1870s to accommodate the slow mechanical movement of early typewriters. It's hardly an efficient design for modern use, when the ability to keyboard is nearly as important as the ability to write.

Dvorak's ergonomic design allows 70% of all typing to be done on the home row (only 32% of Qwerty's keystrokes are on its home row), which helps make typing easier, faster, and — probably (formal studies have yet to be done) — less likely to result in carpal tunnel syndrome and other repetitive motion injuries.

For more information on the Dvorak keyboard, send $2.00 (for

printing and postage) to Dvorak, Freelance Communications, PO Box 17326, Boulder CO 80303 USA, or see our web page: http://www.thisistrue.com/

Get More *True*

This is True compilations come out every year, pulling together a year's worth of Randy's column plus *extra* stories and headlines that didn't fit into his weekly space. Order the books through your favorite bookstore, or get them directly from us. Either way, be sure to "Get One for Every Bathroom in the House!"

• • •

☐ Send me Volume 1! I need ___ copies of *This is True: Deputy Kills Man With Hammer* at $11.00 each plus $2.00 shipping*.

☐ I need ___ more copies of Volume 2, *This is True, Glow-in-Dark Plants Could Help Farmers* for $11.00 each plus $2.00 shipping*.

* Only one $2.00 shipping charge is required per order, no matter how many copies are ordered. (U.S., Canada, FPO/APO only. Offer may be withdrawn at any time. Write for shipping rates for other countries, or see our web page.)

☐ I'm desperate to get a regular *True* fix every week by e-mail. Please e-mail me information on Internet subscriptions!

☐ *This is True* isn't in any newspapers near me, and it should be. I'm attaching the name, address and phone number of a paper near me that needs to carry *True* every week.

• • •

☐ Check or Money Order Enclosed

☐ Charge my: ☐ Visa ☐ Mastercard ☐ Discover ☐ AmEx

Card # _____-_____-_____-_____ (Expires: ___/___)

Name: _____

Address: _____

City: _____ State/Prov: _____

Zip/Postal Code: _____ Country: _____

E-mail address:_____

Mail this form with check or credit card information to Freelance Communications, PO Box 17326, Boulder CO 80308 USA, or fax with your credit card information to +1-500-442-TRUE, or see our web page: http://www.thisistrue.com/